DRAW GREAT

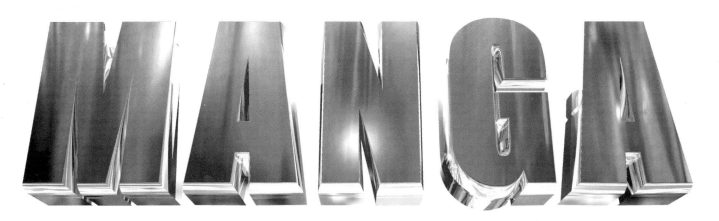

EMMETT ELVIN AND EUGENE FELDER

BARNES
&NOBLE
BOOKS
NEW YORK

Copyright ©2004 by Kandour Ltd UK

This edition published by Barnes & Noble Inc.,
by arrangement with Kandour Ltd UK.

2005 Barnes & Noble Books
Reprinted 2005

M 10 9 8 7 6 5 4 3 2

ISBN 0-7607-6244-9

Printed and bound in India

Created by Metro Media Ltd, UK
Written and illustrated by Emmett Elvin and Eugene Felder
Cover and content design: Eugene Felder and Emmett Elvin
Managing editors: Jenny Ross and Emma Hayley

Contents

Foreword

Back in the late 1980s when I first started reading Manga it had, at best, a cult following. "What's wrong with proper comics?" mainstream comic fans would ask. "Why bother with this Japanese stuff?"

Their mild hostility and confusion was understandable; storylines concerning poison-drinking contests and people who turned into animals when it rained were hardly the stock-in trade of the men-in-tights brigade. But this was what attracted me. I loved the sheer strangeness of those early arrivals to our Western shores. Tales that flew in the face of Western logic and seemed to exist for the pure joy of it, characters and scenarios gloriously unhampered by the conventions of decades of corporate comic formulae.

Now, in the 21st century, Manga is no longer marginalized and misunderstood. Kids have grown up absorbing Manga and anime at their local movie theaters, and this boom has sparked a desire among our burgeoning community to produce our own. These days there's no shortage of how-to and teach-yourself guides, but few address the heart of the matter.

That is exactly the aim of this book, which is our most ambitious yet. It goes beyond the superficial and confronts head-on some of the knottiest problems which plague the budding Manga artist. I'm happy to say that our hard work has paid off and, along the way, it has been a lot of fun.

Application and practice always pay dividends but remember: if it ain't fun, it won't get done.

So: enjoy!

Emmett Elvin

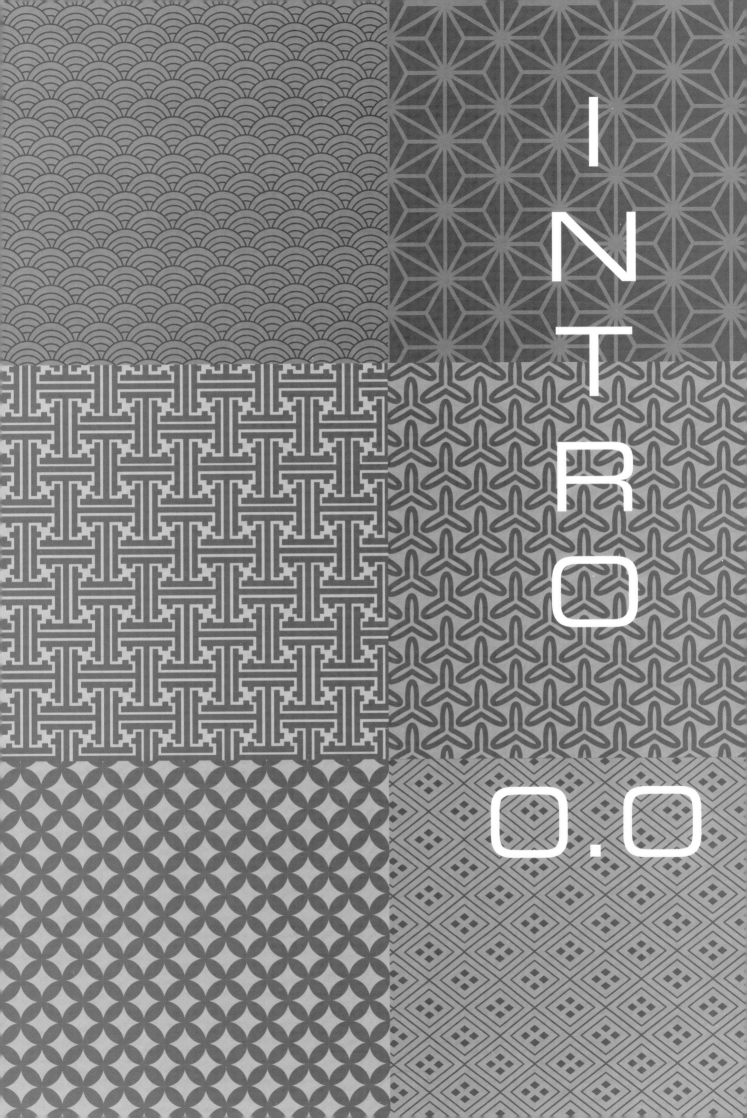

INTRO 0.0

Who is this book for?

This is a very different book from the run-of-the-mill Manga how-tos that you may have read already.

The vast majority of these books maintain a similar formula which asks the reader to follow, or even just copy, a series of steps enabling a reasonable result.

We have aimed a lot deeper. The basics were covered in our book, Beginner's Manga: a Step-by-Step Guide, where we provided readers – regardless of ability – with the principles to get them started. This volume, however, assumes the reader is already familiar with those ideas and is now ready to move onto the next level.

In Draw Great Manga we've abandoned the formulaic approach and opted for an inspirational one, exploring the avenues which have been of personal aid to us, the authors, all the while supplying a wealth of factual instruction.

Add your enthusiasm to our inspiration and solid framework and

there is no reason why you, the reader, should not become a successful Manga artist.

The number one requirement for getting the most out of this volume is the simple desire to improve your skills. That sounds simplistic and obvious, but ultimately your enthusiasm is the make or break factor involved here.

As you will already now know, Manga is a vast subject with a diversity of sub-genres and artistic styles. This book is as inclusive as possible, with no real bias towards any one approach, which means that devotees from cyberpunk to shoujo manga will discover applicable advice and information within these pages.

There are areas which may seem at first glance to be more relevant to anime, such as model sheets and character rotations, but they are hugely beneficial to Manga as well.

A well studied, fully formed character will always be better than one where the first draft has been splurged straight onto the page. Proper character development applies to both Manga and anime, and here we show you the techniques used by the professionals to achieve this. We have included these in chapter 6, along with some other tools which are equally useful in both mediums.

There are also several subjects covered in this volume which you won't find in most entry-level titles:

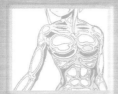

foreshortening, dramatic lighting, extreme perspective and working productively with graphics programs are all techniques which help us make the leap from enthusiastic amateur to confident professional.

These are also the subjects which give the fledgling artist the most headaches, so our brief has been to take the fear out of them and present them in an easy-to-grasp format.

The first two chapters are the weightiest ones. This is where the real meat of the matter is dealt with. Chapter 1 focuses on the main problems encountered when drawing, from anatomy to foreshortening.

Chapter 2 is a more technical chapter. In it we take a good look at how an understanding of basic physics can be of huge benefit to our drawing techniques. It also covers topics such as the behavior of light, perspective and the movement of an object through three dimensional space.

The rest of the book looks at ways of improving our Manga by other means, done largely by employing a number of useful aids.

Use this book as a reference when you are stuck for an approach – it offers a wealth of solutions to a whole host of problems and, as we have said, contains valuable information that you are unlikely to find in other books on the subject.

If you have the desire to elevate your artwork from the fan stage into the professional arena, then this is the book for you.

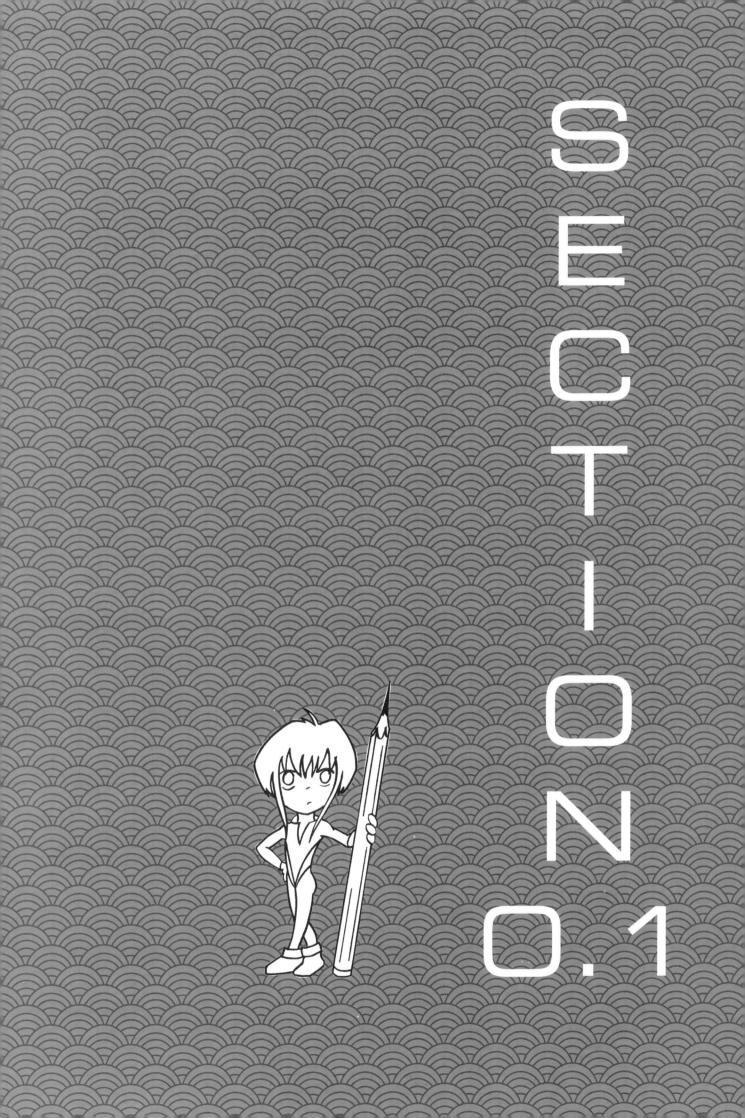

SECTION 01

Drawing to the next level

There are two types of artist. Those who draw purely for the fun of it and those who draw because they are pursuing a level of ever-improving excellence. Both are perfectly valid. After all, didn't we all start drawing because it was fun?

The first type of artist will generally be happy to stay within their perceived limitations, getting enjoyment from what is already familiar territory. The second type, on the other hand, will be on the look out for fresh challenges. These challenges will be at times very demanding, but they know it's worthwhile, as it ultimately adds to their arsenal of knowledge and techniques.

Wouldn't it be great to be able to draw anything that came into your head, the only limit being your imagination? And not only to be able to draw it, but also for it to look exactly as you saw it in your head, with all the design, power and detail you wanted?

This, of course, can take years and years, but is the hallmark of a truly great Manga artist – one who can translate their imaginations straight on to the page, with no compromise.

Needless to say, we can't arrive at that point without setting ourselves meaningful challenges and forcing ourselves to work through difficult problems. This means confronting the things we least like drawing and making them a pleasure. Don't like drawing buildings? Then set yourself the task of becoming expert in drawing them. Hate drawing hands? Make a relentless study of them. Only

by doing this can we become fully fledged artists, scared of nothing and capable of anything.

This first chapter takes a look at what we can do to push the boundaries of our figure drawing. We're going to take in foreshortening, eyes, hair, head shapes and more, but to get us started we'll limber up with some fun and easy stuff, designed to get the hands and mind in the mood for the heavier work.

The working day begins

You've had your coffee and showered. Now it's time to get to work. But your body is still half asleep and the caffeine hasn't reached all of your nerve endings yet.

So, how to get going? Just as athletes never head straight into action, we too should do some limbering up before getting down to the serious stuff.

The following exercises are examples of simple things we can do to get the creative juices flowing. They are not intended to produce awesome visual results. They are purely to get our drawing hands up to speed.

What's the point in this? Moving your pen or pencil in different directions like this is great for getting the wrist and fingers supple. It also helps with mind/hand coordination. Ultimately, there are only two things you can draw: a straight line or a curve. What these end up representing is another matter, but becoming proficient at the very basic level has a positive effect on everything we draw.

Try switching your mind off completely as you do these exercises. Are the results better or worse? You may be surprised.

These exercises are perfect for finding out exactly what we actually know, either instinctively or having learned. They are also good for finding out whether thinking too much is a good idea.

We're not encouraging mindlessness. Far from it. Rather there are some drawing tasks which seem to be better performed by relying on what the hand can do without our brains interfering.

Here's an example: the best way to ink a long, curving line flawlessly is to load up your brush, pen or tool of choice, move it to the starting point and don't look at the brush or pen at all. Instead, look at where you are aiming, and ink the line in one smooth action. Does an archer look at the bow or the target?

There is a Zen Bhuddist practice of circle painting, or Enso, in which the artist creates a perfect circle with one swift brushstroke.

No amount of thought can help us do that.

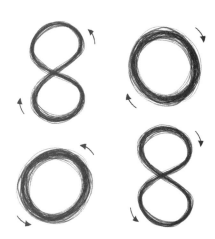

Exercise 1: figure of eight
Repeat a figure of eight pattern several times without lifting your pen or pencil from the page. Do this clockwise first, and then repeat in a counter-clockwise direction.

Exercise 2: circles
Draw 20 circles in one direction and then the other. They will probably improve with each one.

Speed-sketching figures

When we've had enough of circles and started to feel at least a little limbered up, we can move on to some basic, fast figure sketches. You should spend between 20 seconds and a minute on each one. Draw without stopping. If it looks wrong, just start a new sketch. If you find yourself lingering over some detail or making decisions, you are missing the point. In this exercise we are relying purely on the information that is innately within us. Just get a feeling for the figure you want to sketch and go.

DRAWING AUTOMATICALLY

Our knowledge of anatomy should be good enough that once we've seen the pose in our minds, we simply let our hands get on with the job. It can take a long, long time to reach this stage, but it's a great thing to aim for.

HAPPY ACCIDENTS

Sometimes, when working in this speed drawing style, we'll produce an unexpected result that looks great. There will be something about the shape, pose or general dynamic that appeals. Don't let this interrupt your drawing. But do file it to one side for later study. These are the things that really teach us new approaches to drawing.

Anatomy 1:

At right is a fully-boned skeleton. The human skeleton is made up of 179 bones, and, if you don't already know the names of the major bones mentioned at right, it is advisable to learn them, as they will be used in this chapter.

Those you may be less familiar with are mandible (lower jaw), clavicle (collar bone), sternum (center bone of rib cage) and patella (knee cap).

Also study the simplified version of the skeleton, on the facing page, which is perfectly adequate for at least 95% of our Manga drawing. The individual ribs are fused to produce a one-piece chest, which can be expanded or contracted as per our needs. The basic bowl-shape of the pelvis remains, and lower arms and lower legs are simplified into single-bone arrangements.

The skeleton

cranium

mandible

clavicle

rib cage

sternum

upper arm

spine

forearm

pelvis

hand

thigh bone

patella

shin bone

ankle

foot

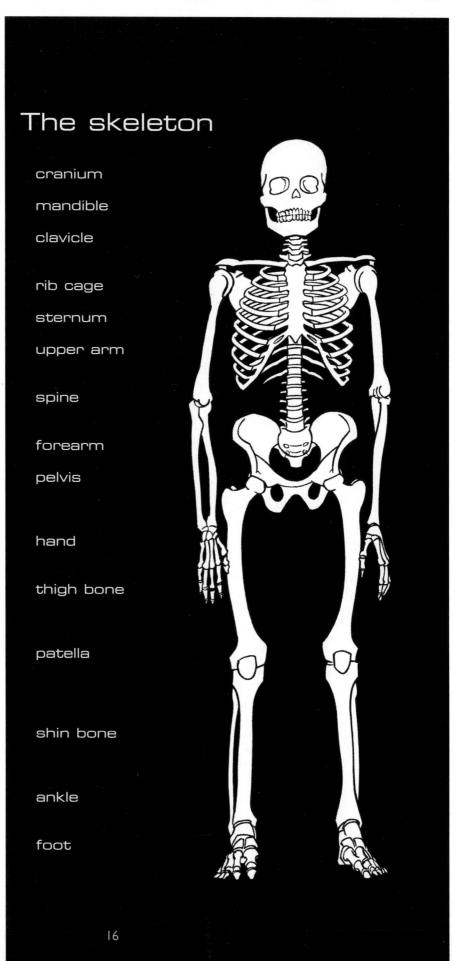

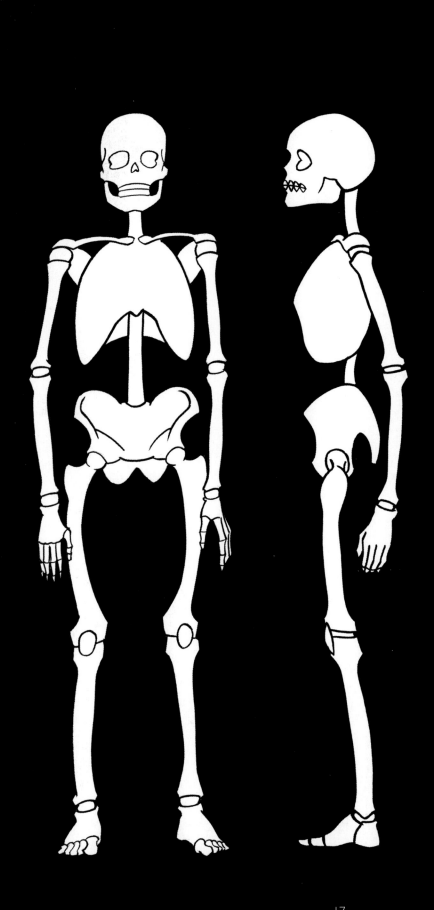

FRONT AND SIDE VIEWS OF OUR SIMPLIFIED SKELETON

Notice how the leg bones bend in two directions. In the frontal view, they bend inward as they move from the pelvis to the knee. In the side view, the bend is backwards towards the knee. This double bend is partly what gives the leg bones the strength they need to support the weight of the body. The same phenomenon is also true of the arm bones, although less noticeable. There are no truly straight bones in the human body.

Unsavory though it may be for the vegetarians among us, a visit to your local butcher or meat market can pay dividends. A thigh bone from a cow will, if properly studied, teach you more about the structure of bones than any book ever could.

Skeleton in action

Let's take our simplified skeleton, invent some poses for him, and see if we can make it run or walk. Try using some of the speed sketch poses from earlier as a framework for skeleton drawing.

Do as many drawings of this as it takes until it becomes second nature to you. It's impossible to overstate the importance of understanding the underlying structure of things. In the case of the human body, this is especially important. We have to learn both the possibilities and the limitations of the human body which, of course, all starts with the bone structure.

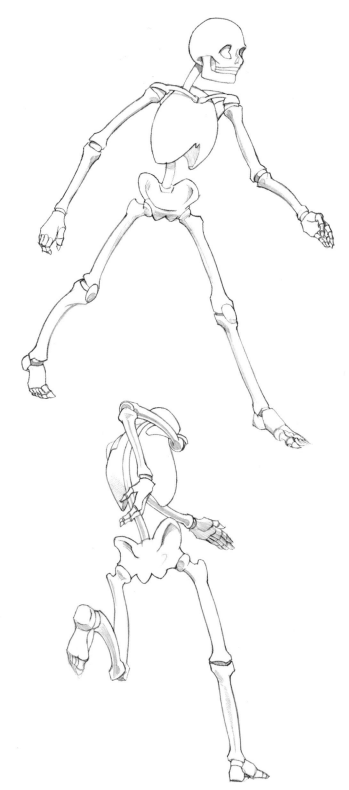

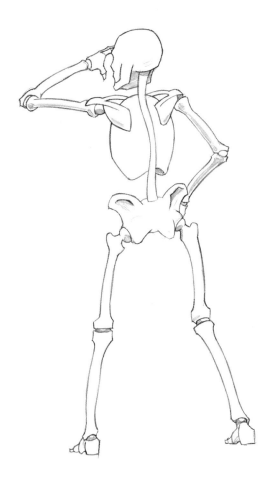

The skull

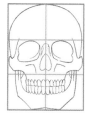

fig. a.

The skull is essentially the framework for the human face, so study it well.

The skull is made up of two parts. The cranium is the brain case and also includes the eyes, nose and upper jaw. The second, smaller part is the mandible, a hinged, extended horseshoe – shaped bone housing the lower jaw.

Heads in Manga vary hugely, from the realistic to the wildly exaggerated, but they are all ultimately based on variations on the regular human skull. Stereotypically Manga head shapes are discussed in more detail later in this chapter.

Viewed from the front, the skull is of a ratio of three x two, i.e. three units high to two units wide. If we divide the skull up in this way we can clearly see three separate sections. The top third is the oval housing for the brain, the middle third the eyes and nose and the bottom third the teeth and lower jaw. See fig. a.

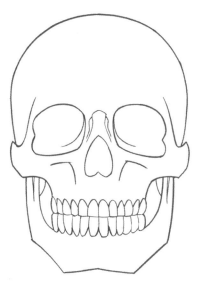

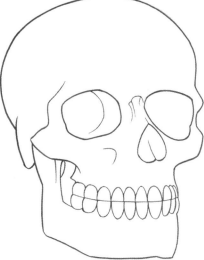

most noticeable features that single out one individual from another.

Due to the unique differences in our skulls – not our muscles – our faces are recognizable, even to people who haven't seen them for a long time. Cheekbones, eyes, jaw size, all these characterizing features and more are dictated by the shape of our skull.

Viewed from the side, the skull can be contained within a perfect square. This is worth remembering, as a common mistake is not drawing the cranium deep enough.

The human face has many small muscles which have a great effect on our expressions. But it's the skull which dictates the

Try drawing the human head from unusual angles, for example from under the chin or looking down at an angle. Doing this will teach us a great deal about the features of the skull and the relationship between them.

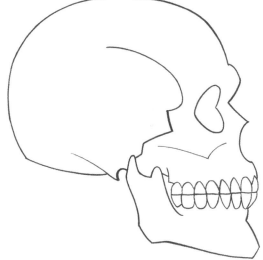

Anatomy 2:

Musculature

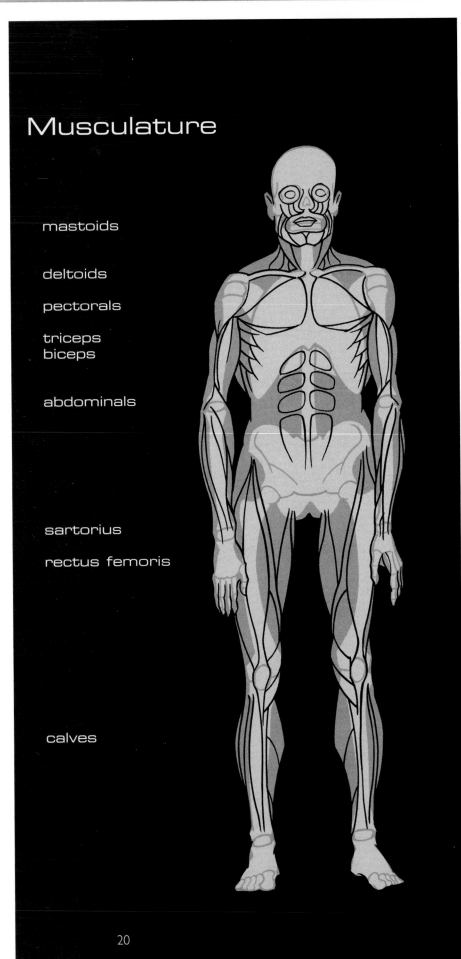

At right is a diagram showing the main muscles in the human body. This has been superimposed over the basic skeleton to demonstrate how one relates to the other. Take time to refer to the diagram below and learn the names of these muscles. The simple act of naming and remembering them helps to build up a more complete working model in our minds.

Simple rules for muscles

1: Every muscle begins somewhere and ends somewhere.

2: The muscles are attached to the bones by ligaments.

3: Muscles tend to widen towards the middle and narrow near the ligaments.

4: The position of the skeleton can completely change the shape of a muscle.

You may be unfamiliar with some of the muscle names. The mastoid muscles run from the ear down to the center of the clavicle. The deltoids are the shoulder muscles. The pectorals, usually called the "pecs," are the major muscles of the chest. When the arm pulls upwards the biceps are brought into action. When pulled downward, the triceps flex. The abdominals are what's more commonly referred to as the "six pack" or stomach muscles. The sartorius is a ribbon-like muscle that runs from the hip down to the inside of the knee. The rectus femoris is the most obvious muscle of the upper front leg and connects to the main tendon of the knee.

mastoids

deltoids

pectorals

triceps
biceps

abdominals

sartorius

rectus femoris

calves

Female or male?

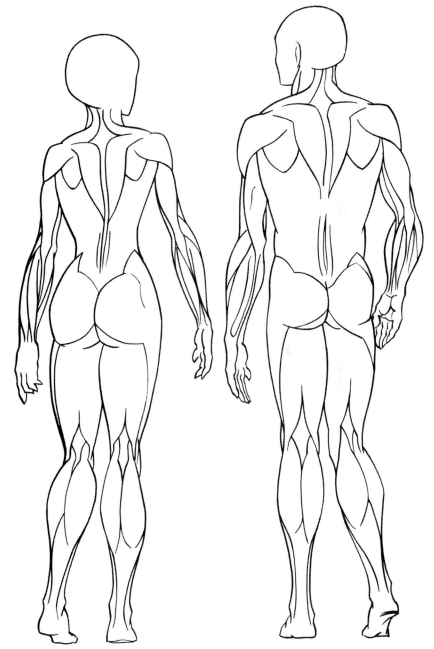

The differences between these two images become glaringly obvious once we add muscle. Starting from the head the female form displays:

- narrower neck
- narrower shoulders
- narrower waist
- wider hips
- smaller hands
- smaller feet
- fewer sharp angles

In comparison, the male figure looks "squared off," lacking many of the gentle curves that the female form exhibits. At its most extreme, it's the difference between elegance and power. This is a useful thing to bear in mind when trying to demonstrate the gender of characters.

Male and female character creation will be discussed in great detail in chapter 6. For now, the general characteristics of muscle construction of both sexes will be considered.

The human body has fast and slow muscle fibers. The first are used for high energy activities such as running and jumping. The slow muscle fibers are concerned with posture and gripping, activities that need slow, sustained energy release.

The male body has a higher proportion of fast muscle fibers, making it appear generally more muscular and powerful. Conversely, the female body tends to have more slow muscle fiber, particularly important for childbirth.

Both muscle types may be developed or allowed to diminish in males or females. This can produce either athletic looking women or on the other hand, less athletic-looking men.

Women also have a natural bias toward subcutaneous fat. This insulating layer lies just below the skin and helps to smooth out the definition of the muscles.

A closer look

Muscles have a tendency to "flow" in and out of each other. This can be clearly seen in the drawing at right. At the point where the deltoid (shoulder), bicep (major arm muscle) and the pectorals (chest muscles) meet they fit tightly together to produce an extremely well-defined area. The points where muscles converge should be given particular attention. Mastering these "hot spots" helps us gain control over the whole body and give figure drawing a conviction otherwise difficult to achieve.

All muscles are essentially a variation on the same theme. Connected to the bones via ligaments, they start small and tough, ballooning out into much softer, blood-filled areas.

Muscles have start and end points. Very often these are at the meeting points of the bone joints. Knees, elbows and ankles have major muscles attached via ligaments, though these are often obscured by other muscles.

The following pages present an overview of the main muscle areas you will need to be familiar with in order to make your Manga characters not only believable but dynamic.

THE TORSO

This area of the body comprises two major sets of muscles, the pectorals and the abdominals.

The top area of the pectorals is attached to the clavicle, though this is too deep beneath the skin to be immediately obvious. However, this does mean that one can't move

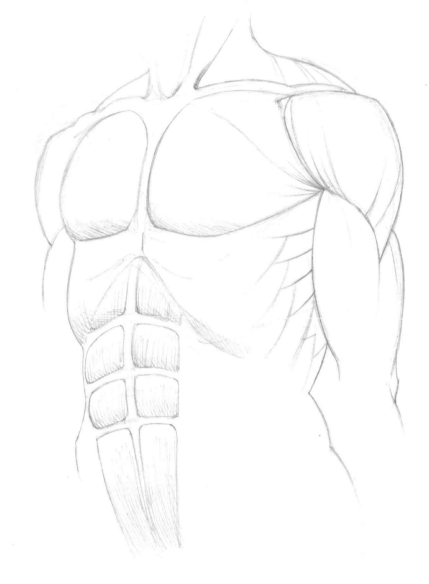

without affecting the other.

They run across the ribs from the shoulder to the sternum and are among the largest muscles of the body.

Even though abdominals are often referred to as the "six-pack," they are actually a collection of eight muscles,

as the above drawing shows. The bottom pair are much less likely to be visible as they are less pronounced.

As these do not run along a bone, their shape can change drastically, depending on the owner's position. Their shape will tend to mirror that of the spine.

What moves what?

There are no truly independant parts in the human body. If one part moves, the chances are that its neighbor will be affected. Such a thought can be a little overwhelming when we first try to build a mental model of the human body in our

raises his arm?

Firstly, the shoulder moves up. And what's attached to the shoulder? Both the pectorals and the clavicle. Compare their positions in both images. Notice the change in angle of

These are some similar questions to consider:

How do the arm muscles change when the wrist is rotated as far as it will go?

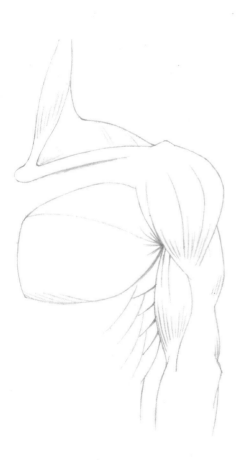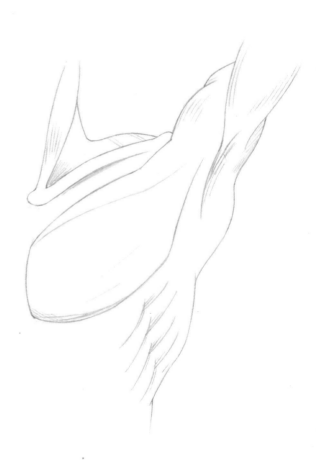

heads. But over time this can be acheived, with a little help from diagrams like the one above.

The image above left shows the shoulder area in a relaxed position. So what will move if the model

the clavicle, the other end of which remains in its original position.

In addition to these changes, there is also a general upwards shift of the muscle mass running from the shoulder to the pelvis.

In what way do the abdominals change shape when the upper body is twisted? Try drawing this.

For first-hand information on this, study your own body and the way muscles move in relation to one another.

BACK

The muscles of the back tend to be either large but flat or long and narrow, running along the spine.

Helpful markers are the shoulder blades. These tend to be visible to some degree at all times.

The image at right shows the relationship between the back muscles and the shoulders. These flat "V" shaped muscles are called the trapezius muscles and join the neck muscles flowing into the shoulder.

When the back is arched, the spinal muscles near the base of the spine can clearly be seen. These muscles follow the spine all the way up to the neck, but are at their most visible at the lower back.

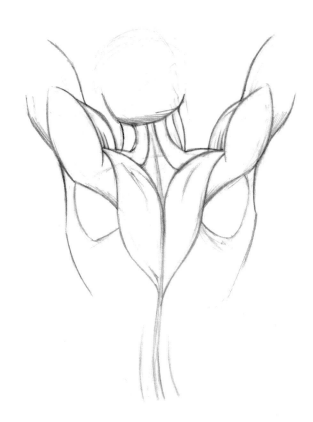

ARMS

The two major muscles of the upper arm are the biceps and the triceps. They perform quite different functions and are relatively independant. The biceps terminate at the elbow via ligaments you can easily feel in your own body.

The forearms are a more complex arrangement with no obviously larger muscles, but instead a collection of small and medium-sized ones.

It's very important to remember that the wrist can be rotated while keeping the elbow in the same position. This results in the forearm muscles twisting as they make their way towards the wrist.

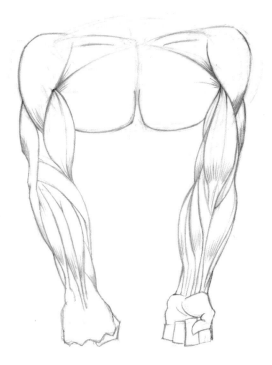

LEGS

The legs are probably the most complex collection of muscles and thus the muscles lazy Manga artists are most likely to invent!

Good areas to concentrate on first would be the calf muscles, the ligaments around the knees and the major muscles at the front of the upper leg, such as the rectus femoris, the large muscle which connects to the major tendon of the knee.

One of these muscles, called the sartorius, runs from the hip diagonally across the front of the leg, ending at the inside of the knee. You can see this quite clearly on the image on page 12.

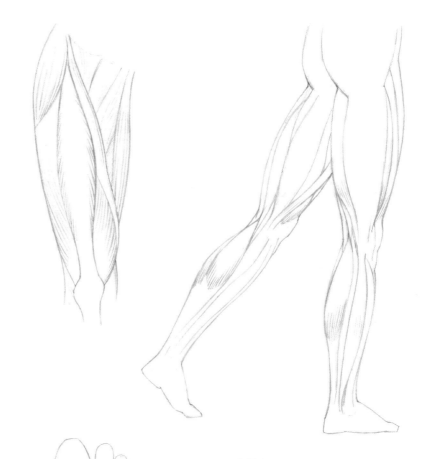

FEET

Often overlooked and by no means easy to get right. This may be because we don't tend to see feet out of shoes that often in Manga.

The main muscles in the feet are at the sole. The upper part is largely bone and ligament.

The tendons on the upper part of the foot usually protrude when the foot is in use, especially the large tendon running from the big toe to the ankle.

If you really want some practice, try drawing a character standing on tiptoes and making them look perfectly balanced – a good challenge even for the experienced artist!

The Hand

The beginner's nemesis. Muscles, tendons, knuckles, bones and skin folds are all in one small, highly adaptable package.

The biggest obstacle to drawing hands successfully is to underestimate their complexity and their possibilities.

Cable-like tendons run from the muscles of the forearm. At the wrist, they pass under a kind of natural tape holding the tendons in place. Those of the middle three fingers extend from a central point and move towards their respective knuckles. The tendon of the little finger runs a separate course (see right). The tendons then continue through to the fingertips. Try feeling your forearm whilst opening and closing your hand.

The significant muscles of the hand are located at the base of the thumb and beneath the little finger at the side of the palm.

WHAT'S OVER THERE?

Once we know the location of the tendons and muscles, the hand becomes something to really add expression to our characters. If hands aren't handled properly characters are robbed of a whole arsenal of gestures and actions.

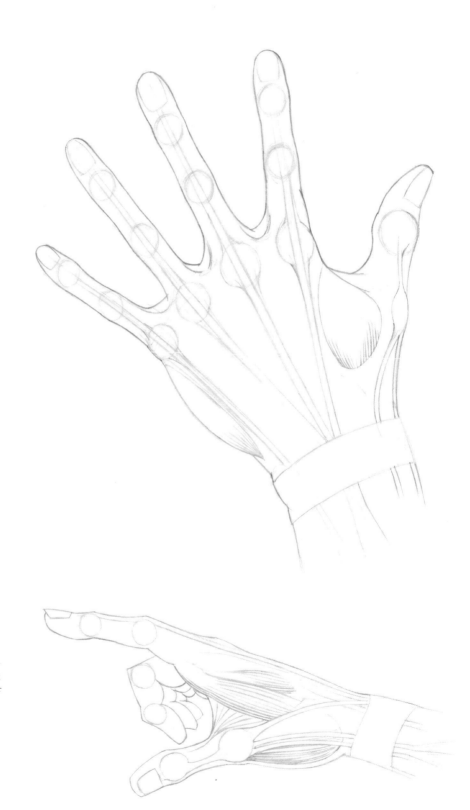

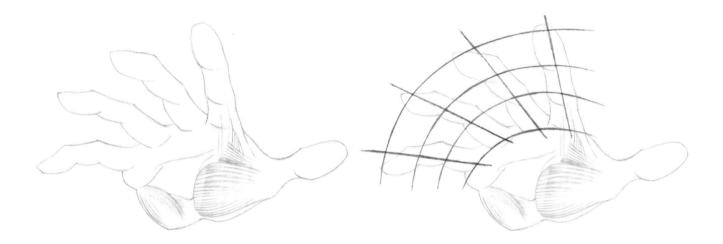

THE SECRET HAND PATTERN

Although we appear to have four independent fingers, they almost always move in *patterns*. What this means is we can use very regular guides to show their relationships.

In the image above, we have four fingers partly splayed out. This means they are all facing in slightly different directions but with a definite pattern to their positioning.

By drawing arcs through the knuckles of this hand we can see an undeniable relationship. At top right is the "map," showing clearly the logic behind this seemingly complex pose.

The simple fact is that the hand works best when the digits all function as a group, not individually.

Knowing this secret also allows us to make sure that all our hand drawings have strength and realistic structure.

Why not experiment with drawing your own hand in various positions, always looking out for the all-important arc pattern?

GOING TO EXTREMES

We can become expressive with our hands by pushing their capabilities to the limit, or even slightly beyond.

These three images show hands at or near the limits of their bendability. If we go much beyond this, believability begins to disappear.

A good rule is, the more cartoony your Manga, the more you can get away with breaking the laws of nature.

Foreshortening

Foreshortening can be used to show objects realistically when viewed at extreme or unusual angles.

Examine the components in any picture and see them only from the perspective we are trying to draw.

The brain has a habit of automatically picturing objects from the most easily recognizable angle. For example, when a gun is suggested, it will usually be visualized from side on. A violin is viewed not from the side, but rather front on, showing the instrument's distinctive shape. You should try and avoid this tendency.

At right are three images of the same banana. Side, three-quarters and front views are shown, allowing us to observe the line of the curves. Have a good look at the curve that runs along the middle of the top banana. By the time we get to the third image, something slightly unexpected has happened: what started out as a nice, smooth, uninterrupted curve is now two curves going in different directions.

With more involved images, it is difficult to correctly guess the behaviour of the lines and curves involved. This is why the study of foreshortening is essential.

The key to accurate foreshortening is knowing which direction the curvature is in. We know that no bone in the body is truly straight, so by increasing the curve of the bone, or banana for that matter, we can make the image believable.

Another aspect we have to consider

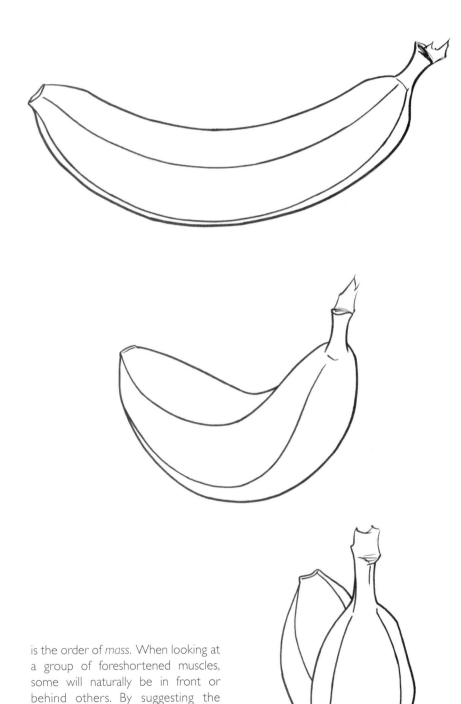

is the order of *mass*. When looking at a group of foreshortened muscles, some will naturally be in front or behind others. By suggesting the contours of the musculature in the right order we can create very convincing body shapes.

BEYOND BANANAS

Let's use a very common Manga pose as an exercise: the classic image of a gun pointing almost directly at the viewer. We'll make things harder for ourselves still by making the forearm naked, so no unidentified bits of jacket can help hide mistakes. The muscles of the forearm, if drawn correctly will help the viewer read the picture.

Make a fresh study of the three component parts; the forearm, the hand and the gun, but seen front on.

Do as many studies as it takes before committing a reasonable drawing from memory. The better the planning is, the less mistakes are likely to be made in the finished drawing, and thus the quicker it is executed. It is far better to make errors at the study stage when it doesn't really matter. At the final stage, this could be disastrous.

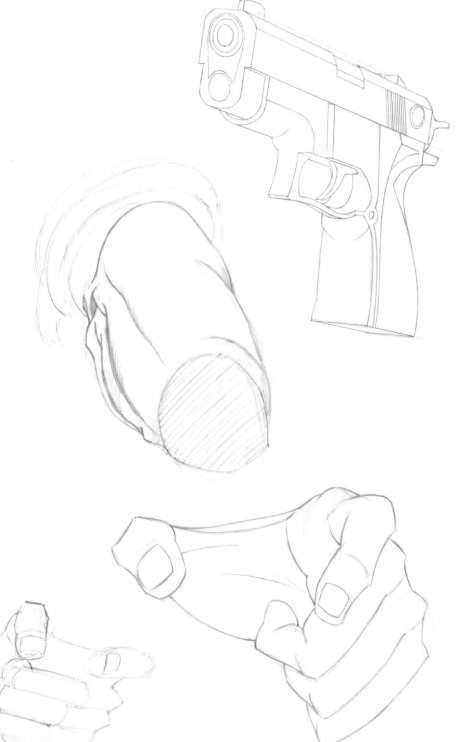

To create the image put the parts together:

Block out the major shapes of the foreshortening. With a head-on shot, assume a roughly square shape to contain the elements of the arm and gun. This is shown at right.

Unless we determine the space occupied by the components at the start, there is a good chance the elements will not stay in proportion, and the drawing will be unsuccessful. Containing them beforehand precludes this.

When the main shapes and sizes of the gun, hand and forearm are satisfactory, begin adding the other elements of the image, paying attention to the scale of the head, shoulders and the other hand and the forearm.

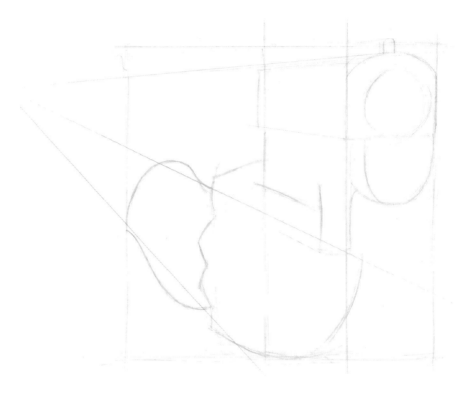

Opposite is the final result. By throwing in speedlines to maximize the drama, a truly in-your-face image is achieved.

For the record, Eugene's arm was sketched as a preliminary and I sketched my own hand. A cheap plastic pistol was used as the basis for the gun, on to which I added details of a Browning automatic from images found online.

Try some extreme foreshortening on furniture, stairs, animals and anything else that has an interesting and therefore challenging shape. You'll be a better Manga-ka for it.

The Manga head

Over the several decades of Manga's evolution, there have been many innovations contributing to the uniqueness of the form. Perhaps the most immediately obvious is the way the eyes are usually, though not always, larger than life.

Back in the early 80s, there seemed to be a race on to see who could create the biggest, cutest, wettest eyes. This would not be possible without some fairly major modification to the human head. Above right shows what happens when we try to fit a pair of Shoujo Manga style eyes into a regular human head. The results are neither pretty or cute.

The essential problem here is the width of the head. It simply isn't wide enough to capacitate big eyes without forcing them too close together. The trick with the modern Manga head is to have the eyes as big as you like, all the while maintaining a sizable gap between them.

At right is a generic Manga head shape. It's very wide at the temples, but with a comparitively small area for the facial features. Taking this as a starting point, we can squash or stretch as our needs require to achieve a wide variety of head shapes.

This head is about as narrow as it can be, whilst still keeping a good gap between the eyes.

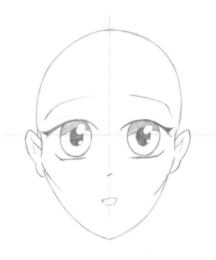

The unfortunate result of trying to fit Manga eyes in a Western shaped head.

In profiles, the jaw area is always further out than the forehead, even on semi-realistic heads.

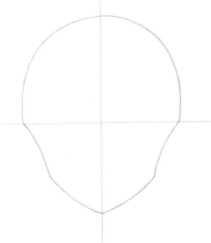

This head shape is a good starting point. With just a little modification it can used to produce the majority of Manga head types.

On less realistic heads the effect can be a lot more extreme, making an almost canine profile.

STYLES

ADULT

This head type will be recognizable from a lot of anime shows, usually depicting quite neutral characters. A good general purpose, if not particularly exciting shape.

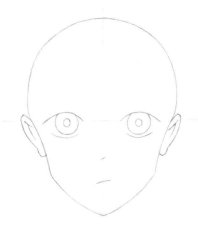

KAWAI

In the kawai babylike face the eyes have been moved downwards, concentrating the features towards the bottom of the head. The jawline has also been rounded for a softer, cuter feel.

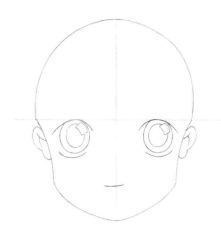

ALMOND

By keeping the eyes where they are and extending the chin down, an older, more masculine face is created. This is a good model for males of 14 and up.

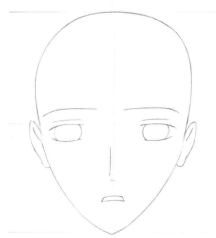

LET'S PUSH IT FURTHER

If the basic Kawai shape is squashed down even more, we can produce some extreme, super-cute faces. These heads are actually wider than they are tall.

HEROES AND VILLAINS

Starting with the almond shaped head, the chin is squared off to make more powerful looking characters. For extra strength, make sure you attach a good, thick neck!

HOW EXTREME?

Faces can be pushed to pretty extreme limits only if the rules of proportion are obeyed. This means maintaining a balance between head width and eye size. As a guide, the bigger the eyes, the less room we have to play with regarding the nose and mouth.

Hair

HAIR HAS SHAPE TOO

Hair cannot simply sprout out at random from the scalp. Human hair has a very definite shape and pattern which needs to be understood before attempting elaborate hairdos. Hair also has it's own behavior and there are definite do's and don'ts.

CLUMPING

As a general rule, the thicker the hair, the more likely it will form into "clumps," the more extreme examples of which can be seen in Manga such as *Dragonball*.

Conversely, thinner hair tends to lie more flatly against the head.

For males, the area around the temples changes with age, as this is the first area to recede. This can be a good way to subtly indicate age in older characters.

Older characters tend to go gray at the temples too.

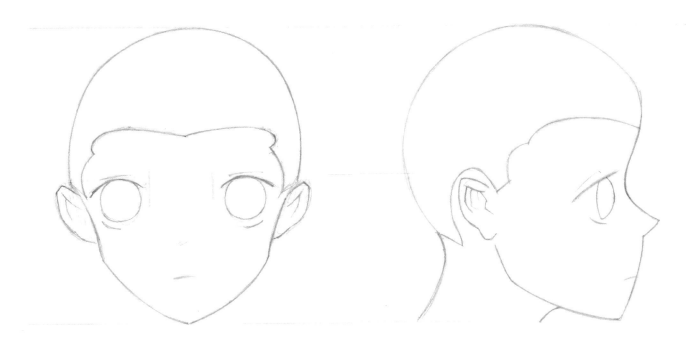

THE PATTERN OF THE HAIR

The above drawings show the outline of the limit of the hair. No matter how bushy and luxuriant the locks, no normal human grows hair outside of this range.

The hair grows outward from the crown, the area roughly at the top of the head.

FOLLOW THE HEAD

To a great extent, the shape of the head plays a big part in the shape of the hair. Hair drawn with no regard for this will nearly always look wrong.

Of particular importance is the area around the ear – see in the above right drawing. The hair avoids going anywhere near the ear, leaving a naked area around it.

FROM REAL TO UNREAL

Although hair in Manga is often wildly unrealistic, it's still a good idea to check out hair in the real world. It's here that we get the information that allows us to experiement with our Manga hairstyles. Pay attention to the reality which Manga imitates and then goes beyond: shine, clumping, anti-gravity effects and wild color.

Styles

At right is a girl whose hair is long, but not particularly thick. As a result, it doesn't defy gravity like thicker hair might, but flows downward from her crown. The hair also forms a central shape between her eyes. This is a common device in Manga for giving hair form, instead of just hanging at random.

Below left is a girl with thicker hair. It stands up along the center before gravity forces it back down. The lines become more vertical as they move towards the crown, helping the hair make visual sense.

Bottom left is a very "clumpy" effect. The white lines have been left in purely to show the construction of this *Dragonball* style hair. Although the hair is sticking out at all angles, there is logic, with the hair growing from a central point, first upwards and then falling as the hair moves down the scalp.

SUPER-SLICK HAIR EFFECTS

Here's a common Manga trick for making straight, black hair look super-glossy:

Step 1. Once we've established the shape of the head, draw contour lines to indicate the position of the highlight effect. These lines must follow the shape of the head if they are to look convincing.

Step 2. Use several lines to indicate the curve of the hair as it moves towards the crown. These will be used as our guides.

Step 3. Ink the head, leaving the highlight area until last. If you don't, it will be hard to guage when the effect is complete. Now use quick brush/ pen strokes to begin putting in the hair lines.

Step 4. The amount of lines you put in depends on how much light you need to reflect. This will be dependent on the character's location, strength of light source, etc.

You will probably need to experiment several times with this technique before you obtain the results you want. Once you've got it, you should be able to bypass stage two and ink without guides.

This technique works well when the hair is super straight, but what if the hair is not? Most of our characters are likely to have less slick hairstyles. The next technique is the one most commonly used in Manga to achieve hair shine for normal hairstyles:

step 1

step 2

step 3

step 4

We don't need to be as exacting with this method, as the hair is looser and more clumped.

Work out roughly where your light source is and put in a couple of rough contour lines. Then draw in the shine lines as below.

Notice that the bottom row of zig-zag lines follow the pattern of the upper ones. This should form a succession of "V" shapes. The effect is unlikely to work if the upper and bottom lines are out of synch.

Below is the final result. If the overall shape is still giving you trouble, imagine the character is wearing a headband, and use this as your contour guide.

Eyes

No popular art has devoted so much time to the creation of the perfect pair of peepers as Manga, so it's only right that we should take a proper look at the techniques employed.

UNDERSTANDING THE EYE

Gather as much information from the real world as possible. Let's look at the eye's construction (fig. a).

Constructing an eyeball
1: Take a white sphere as a starting point (step 1).

2: Cut out 1/8th of the sphere, making a slight indent. If you're having difficulty visualizing this, imagine a spoon gouging a similar shape out of mousse (step 2).

3: Color this concave part, then put a hole in the center (step 3).

4: Encase the whole thing in a glass sphere (step 4).

The result is that we now have all the white part of our eye at the surface of the glass sphere, while the colored part (iris) is set back from the remainder. In reality, the "empty" part of the sphere is filled with a super-clear liquid called aqueous humor.

Notice that the indent, and also the eyelid, cast a shadow at the top of the iris. This helps to give the eyes depth, especially if we add a highlight or two over that part.

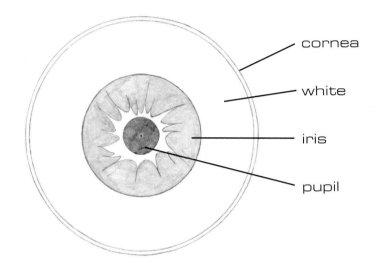

fig. a. The components of an eyeball

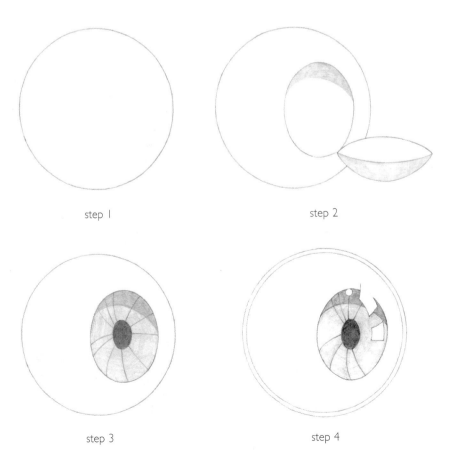

step 1

step 2

step 3

step 4

Here's how we create the Manga equivalent: simply cut more off than 1/8th at step two (fig.a). Try 1/4. Fig. b shows the result of the new, larger iris.

If you want to get a better understanding of the effects of enlarging the iris, take a look at a cat's eyes. If you examine them from the side you'll see how far back their irises are.

You can learn a lot about eyes from studying other mammals. The smaller the mammal, the bigger, proportionately, the iris and pupil.

Now let's put the new, 3D eyes in a Manga model and draw a face in a 3/4 pose:

As you may have figured out, this is another example of how the rules have been changed slightly for Manga. Because the irises are set further back, in fact nowhere near the surface of the eye's outer sphere, we have to be extra careful in these kind of shots. Keep in mind the placement of the

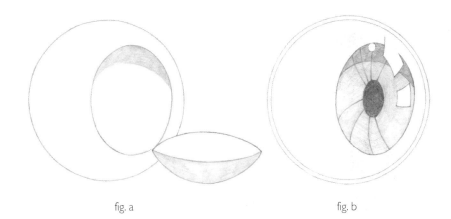

fig. a   fig. b

eyes too: although the eye nearest us is quite close to a standard front view, the other eye is not quite on the same plane. This means the pupil will be more of an oval in the further eye.

If you've managed to draw this view convincingly, you've conquered one of the toughest aspects of drawing the human face. But always observe other people's eyes, ears, noses etc, though try not to stare too hard at strangers.

One may spend years thinking we know how the various parts of the body fit together and work, only to find that on just an afternoon's impartial observation, a lot of our ideas are inaccurate or just plain wrong. Once we attain the reality, we can then warp and mutate it to fit our artistic needs in a completely convincing way.

Eye design

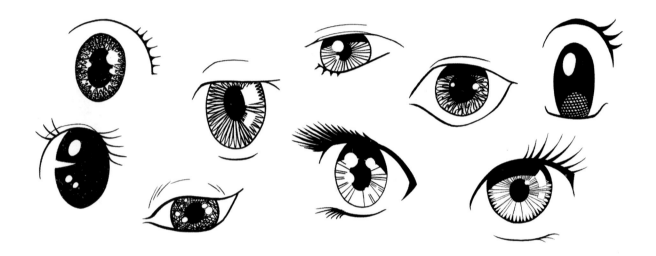

SOME APPROACHES TO EYES

Every Manga artist has their own way of rendering eyes. Some are incredibly detailed, others are beautiful in their simplicity.

The eyes above have been rendered in pure ink, so no tone sheets or computer graphics are involved. We should be able to draw great looking eyes without resorting to such things. In chapter three however, we'll do just that. But for now, try capturing the essence of a Manga eye using pure black.

These component parts need to be considered:

• eyelashes
• whites
• iris
• pupil
• highlights
• shadow

To begin with draw large enough to give yourself the room to experiment. Vary the position and type of highlights you use, and play around with iris size.

Note: when designing eye shapes, the bottom eyelash should always line up with the top eyelash, even if the connection between them is absent. The reader's eye will fill in the gap.

Shape and expression

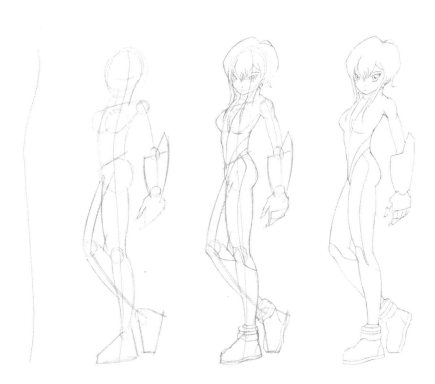

Knowing anatomy inside out, drawing the most ultra-realistic eyes the world has ever seen and foreshortening the most complex character at the most extreme angle imaginable is not enough to be a good Manga artist.

We've all seen drawings that are technically amazing but ultimately leave us with a feeling of "so what?" Why is this? What do they lack?

Life, energy and expression. These are essential elements in Manga, but at the same time are very difficult to teach. This is largely because this is the most instinctive aspect of drawing, and also the most personal.

Most of the expression and shape in artwork is laid down in the first strokes of our pencils. If we can

capture the essence of what we are attempting to portray at this early stage, there's a good chance we'll have a good or even great drawing when we're through.

First we get a feeling for what it is we want to express. With that in mind, start to lay down the essence, or shape of the thing you're trying to capture.

The drawings above and at right show the stages of this, from the first pencil stroke. This first line is an expression of the playful femininity sought here. Then start to block out the major physical elements, all the time holding in mind what is being aimed for. The rest should be just clean up and detail.

41

Breakdowns and finishes

Here is a selection of two-stage drawings. All of the breakdowns were drawn with fast, expressive lines and zero attention to detail.

This demonstrates that a body is, at it's core, a simple shape. At the breakdown stage, a body is not a collection of arms, legs, hands etc. It only becomes that when the details are in place.

If we want to capture someone running, we should find the perfect freeze-frame moment. In the drawing at right, the runner is at his most unbalanced. He has to be running fast in order to avoid falling over! In choosing this moment, we've captured some of his energy.

From life

Some budding artists find drawing from life nothing but a chore. They think it has little or nothing to do with Manga and thus is a waste of valuable drawing time.

Not so.

Reality is full of the unexpected. Not only can it teach us what objects and people actually look like, it can do so in a way that in turns baffles, infuriates, shocks and thrills.

This also forces us outside a limited visual vocabulary and enables us to be completely honest with our subjects and ourselves.

Everytime we sit in a coffee shop or in a park and sketch people, we find something new about the world we live in. A new detail about how jackets hang on people, maybe how evening shadows fall across people's faces or how we look when we are asleep.

When the great anime director Haiyo Miyazaki wants to animate an important scene involving an animal, he doesn't just tell his animation team how to do it. He takes them to the zoo or to a vet and tells them to watch and take notes.

This is what we are doing when we draw from life; adding to our mental library which gives us power to convince the reader that what they are seeing is really happening.

Once again, it's not about making something realistic – it's about making it believable.

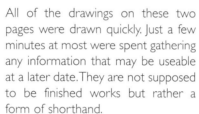

All of the drawings on these two pages were drawn quickly. Just a few minutes at most were spent gathering any information that may be useable at a later date. They are not supposed to be finished works but rather a form of shorthand.

It may be that we incorporate something from a sketch like these years after we first drew them. This often happens without our even

knowing it, bubbling up as it does from our unconscious minds.

When drawing from life try to avoid unnecessary detail. On the facing page, there are two images of a crouching woman in a raincoat from behind. One of them is unsuccessful. Contrary to what you may think, it's the one on the left. This drawing is overworked with needless shadowing and hair detail. All that was needed for this drawing was the shape, which the sketch on the right captures perfectly adequately.

Different guages of pen have been used to produce these drawings. Using a larger guage pen can be an advantage when countering the urge to put in needless detail. This way we obtain what's important. It may not make such a pretty drawing, but that's not the point.

Sketch family members and friends and better still, join a life drawing class, as this encourages regular practice.

Finishing up

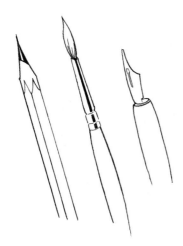

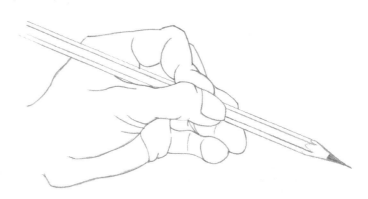

THE PENCIL IN YOUR HAND

Usually when a child draws, chances are they'll be bent over the paper with their faces close to it, tongues poking out and pencil held right next to the tip.

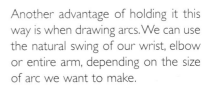

When we see a professional at work it's a different picture. The pencil is held in a way that allows both expression and control, the eyes are far enough away from the paper to get a good overall view and the

tongue pokes out a little less often.

The only time we ever need to hold a pencil anywhere near it's tip is to work on detail. The rest

of the time we should hold it somewhere near the center of the shaft. This allows us maximum control and expression. The pencil is effectively locked in place, so when we draw longer lines, it won't wobble.

Another advantage of holding it this way is when drawing arcs. We can use the natural swing of our wrist, elbow or entire arm, depending on the size of arc we want to make.

In this way we can get the most out of the mechanics of our hand and arm and begin to draw with much greater confidence and expression.

LOOK WHERE YOU'RE GOING

As we mentioned at the beginning of this chapter, the ideal way to draw is to just let your hands do the mechanical part of the job. This means trusting the equipment and your hand to draw effortlessly.

It can take a lot of experience before we can reach the stage where we know exactly what the result of our brush or pencil stroke will be before we even do it. But this is nothing more than a combination of practice and the desire to continually challenge ourselves.

And finally

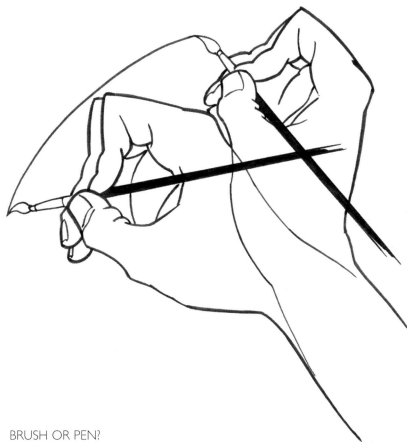

To build confidence try this exercise:

Mark two points on a piece of paper four to five inches apart. Then try to draw a perfect arc between the two, using the methods already described. When you're happy with that, double the distance and do the same thing. Keep increasing the distance between the two points.

The key to this is not to look at what you are doing. Look only at where you're going. This can be a strange concept to grasp at first, but provided your hand is in the right position to start with, you don't need to see what you are drawing, only where you are drawing the line *to*.

This can be especially important when inking, as we only get one chance to get the line perfect. This very fact can sap confidence and make the line feeble or even wobbly. But confidence must be maintained, and the best way is to avoid caution and just do it.

BRUSH OR PEN?

The tool used for inking is a matter of personal preference. A wider variety of line width is obtained with a brush, but a pen is often better for techniques such as cross-hatching, feathering, etc. This book was inked with roughly 70% brush and 30% pen.

BE CLEAN

Make sure your hands are completely clean when you work with inks. It makes a huge difference to inking a strong clean line. Your hand should glide across the paper with a minimum of friction.

Don't attempt to ink anywhere near a recently inked area. It makes a lot more sense to have several ink jobs on the go at once. This way you can work on other pieces as the previous ones are drying which makes good use of time. An ugly smudge is usually the price paid for impatience.

Keep your pencils sharp, your pens and brushes clean and practice until it hurts.

SECTION 0.2

Let's get technical

Learn all the rules.

Then forget all the rules.

These are the two basic laws of all art, and Manga is certainly no exception. We've all found ourselves at some point bogged down with a drawing problem that takes way too long to solve. Why should this be? How can we avoid this happening? Simple. By learning the technical aspects of the subject.

This really is the best way of getting our heads around three-dimensional space.

It is very important to keep in mind that the content of this book cannot be truly learned by simply reading or just looking at the diagrams and images. Real understanding only comes through the experience of *doing*. Sometimes it's easy, other times frustratingly difficult, but everything here will add to your grasp of the world and so make your Manga ever better.

This is where we tackle perspective, light, movement and rotation. Before we can do that, though, we need to take a look at the basics, the shapes that underpin our world.

Some Manga artists started their careers as architects or technical draughtsman. Does this give them an unfair advantage? You bet it does. But following this chapter closely will give you the technical detail you need to create landscapes, buildings and anything else your imagination allows, with all the believability of your favorite Manga-kas.

The nuts and bolts

We've all seen images similar to the ones to our right. They're usually found in manuals for draughtsmen, design blueprints, etc. But what do they represent? They certainly aren't realistic and aren't meant to be. They in fact have more in common with graphic design. As maps of objects they are totally precise, providing the exact and specific information needed to build the depicted form.

With the four images, there is essentially nothing we do not know about this particular nut and bolt. We can recreate it from any angle we choose.

The bottom right image is known as an isometric drawing and is the odd one out. This is because it is not absolutely necessary and gives us no information we can't get from the other three images. However, it is a useful tool as it allows our mind to quickly "connect the dots" and "see" the object's structure in three dimensions. Isometric drawings are made using 30 degree angles, as this is generally considered to give the most realistic looking view, while keeping the drawing mathematically exact. Other views are: axonometric (45 degrees), and oblique (30 or 45 degrees), but these are less relevant here.

The other three images are known as elevations and may be called front, top and side elevations. In the case of a bolt, it makes little difference which elevations we assign to which view. If we were designing a building however, these would have to be correctly assigned, if only to avoid our building being erected upside-down.

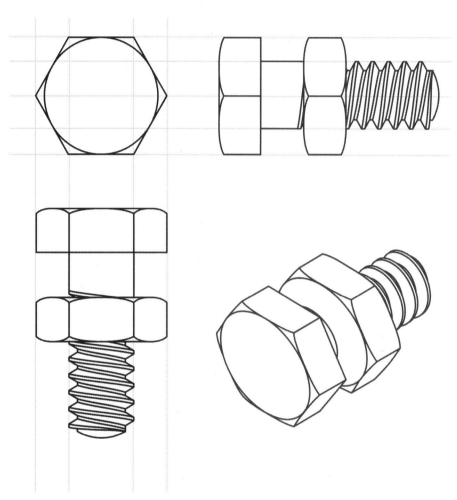

Pick a simple, everyday household object and try drawing precise elevations of it. This teaches us a lot about the three-dimensional nature of the things we see around us. Don't try and draw these things realistically. The point of the exercise is to get a real understanding of the actual structure. Surface detail at this stage is just a distraction, and a distraction we'll get around to later in the chapter. If you draw a can, forget about the label.

This exercise also provides accuracy and good drawing practice. If a professional draughtsman draws, say, an exploded view of an engine, but smudges the ink on one tiny part of the carburettor, the drawing has to be abandoned and restarted.

It is of course possible and even commonplace for these types of drawings to be made with computers. For the Manga artist trying to understand form, the only way to do it is by hand. In doing so, we get all the information hot-wired into our brains.

The cube explored

Here's another way of looking at a three-dimensional object, this time contained within a cube. The six elevations are projected onto their respective sides. This can clearly be seen in the larger, exploded view.

You'll recognize the three bolt elevations from the previous page, here on the sides of the cube. This is exactly what the elevations represent. Any object rotated 90 degrees, either vertically or horizontally forms a "cube" of images, exactly as depicted at right.

Although it may not seem so at first, this is very powerful information. Any thing we can do with a cube – i.e. rotation or perspective – we can do with any other object. All we have to do is understand how it fits into the cube.

Cubes are among the simplest three-dimensional shapes. As such, they are great tools for helping us understand the principles of moving any object through three-dimensional space. Not only that, they are also the only geometric shape we can use to perform this. Using any other shape would produce near-chaos.

Cubes are ideal for this because they have equal sides with equal angles, guaranteeing consistency, no matter how we manipulate them. They are the reason the elevations on the previous pages are drawn the way they are.

The real beauty of this is that ultimately, the math isn't important to learn. Anyone who can draw a cube can work out an object's elevations.

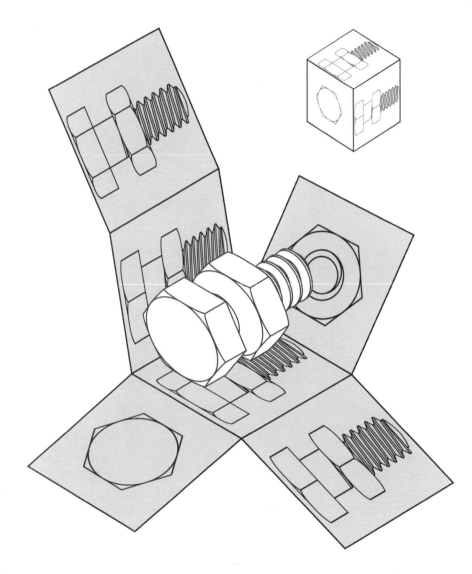

No math whatsoever is necessary to then project that object into three-dimensional space.

Being able to do anything we feel like with any object we want is really the best reason possible to spend some time on this. There are plenty of examples of this coming up on the following pages.

As a tip: finding the center of a cube is easy. The center is located where any two longest diagonal lines intersect. On the small cube above, the top left corner to the bottom right and the top right to the bottom left will intersect at the center.

Rotation explained

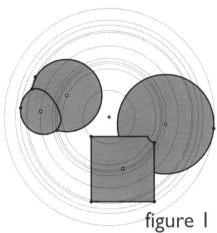

figure I

+   axis of rotation

o   object center

●   furthest orbital points

The above diagram shows a collection of simple shapes as a plan view. As such, they are viewed directly from above.

The concentric circles are a map of the route taken by the orbital points. Because the objects are rotating on a central axis of rotation, and not their own centers, their orbital points describe perfect circles. These circles can never be any larger or smaller.

Because of this, the circles also define the limits of where an object can be. This helps us to work out an object's exact placement. Constrained as it is by the circle of orbit, any given point can only be in one place, and one place only. Once we understand this, the rotation of any given object becomes a lot simpler.

The image to the right may appear to be baffling. But it is really pretty simple to work out when we know what it

represents. The top left section shows the same group of shapes, but instead of a plan view, this time we have a side elevation. There are also three axii: 90 degrees, 45 degrees and 0 degrees (x, y and z). All three pass through one central point. The other three diagrams represent the result of rotation on these axii, with all the objects having been rotated 90 degrees.

The gray lines represent the lines of orbit from fig 1, only this time viewed from different elevations. If we follow the orbital points, we can see these

form straight, parallel lines. They are also always perpendicular to the axis. The 45 degree angle proves an important point: once we understand everything we've discussed here we can put our axis at any angle we want.

Now we understand the nuts and bolts diagram. We understand why the elevations are always at 90 degrees and that this is because we are in fact cubing an object. We also understand the gray lines perpendicular to the axis of rotation represent the orbits of individual points. It's time for some fun.

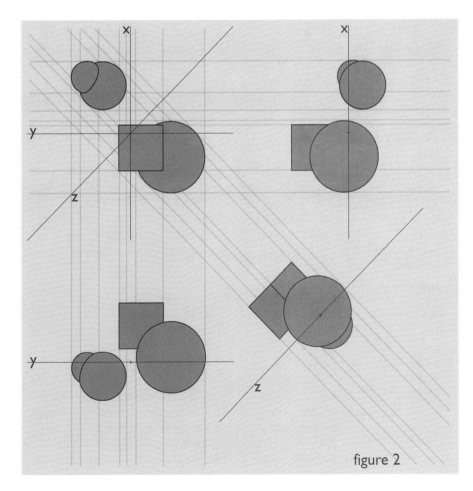

figure 2

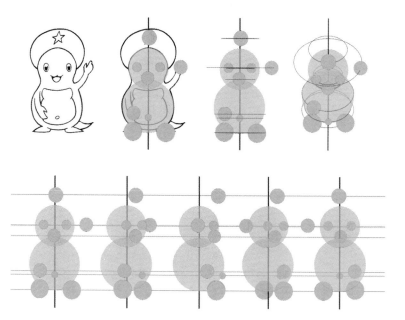

Now let's use those principles for something a little more Manga. We'll rotate the cute, if slightly irritating character to our right. In fact, let's rotate him until he feels nauseous.

The top row shows a construction breakdown. The character's key points are mapped out in simple shapes. Perpendicular to the axis, we draw the gray lines showing the orbit paths. We end with a 45 degree forward tilt, purely to show the orbits involved.

At right, we see the orbital paths extended across the width of the image, forming guidelines for the character's 180 degree rotation.

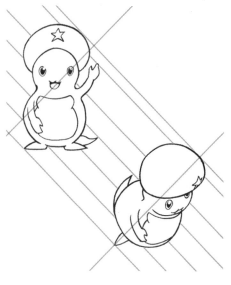

Above is the "real world" rotation of the character. The guidelines are in exactly the same place, but our creature is no longer a collection of gray spheres.

This is the usual way a character is rotated for a "turnaround" – the guide sheets for Manga and anime characters. But what if we want to rotate him at a different angle? This will be a lot harder as we have to stop thinking in terms of facial features etc and get back into the theory of it. With an angle like this,

there's no hiding place!

The drawing to the left shows the result of changing a 90 degree axis to a 45 degree one. But it needn't stop there! Why not try a 30 degree rotation? Or a 80 degree one? At times, you may feel like your brain is going to burst, but the end results can be very satisfying.

After doing enough of this, you'll be able to dispense with a lot of the guidelines and rotate with a bare minimum of framework.

Complexity from simplicity

The four cubes above are the framework for all of the following drawings, with the exception of the four at bottom right.

The first cube is a simple wireframe. The second is with solid sides. The third has diagonal lines pinpointing the center of the top plane. The

of the top plane. We begin with an equilateral pyramid, i.e. a four-sided shape whose angles and sides are all the same. With each step, we increase the number of vertical sides, always keeping the shapes farthest points within the dimensions of the cube. Using this method we move from a crude pyramid through to a cone.

On the third tier the same principle is used, only this time we begin with a

five-sided shape constructed from three square sides and two equilateral triangles. This is the simplest shape we can start with in order to evolve it through to a perfect cylinder, the final image in the series.

At bottom right is a selection of reasonably complex shapes, none of which fit conveniently into a cube. It can be done, but for most purposes a sphere would make a perfectly good substitute.

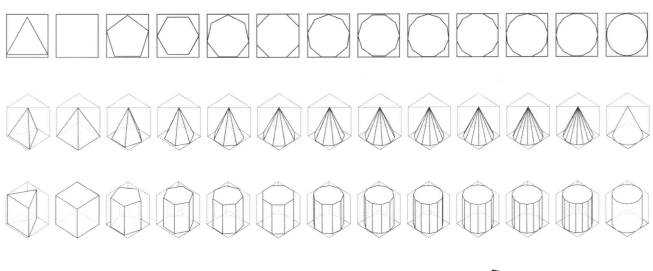

fourth shows a view with the top and nearest two sides removed.

Above are diagrams showing the evolution of a three-dimensional shape. In the first tier, a plan view, we can see it change from the simplest form, a three-sided pyramid, to a shape with such complexity that it is indistinguishable from a circle.

The second tier shows us a view from 45 degrees above the horizontal. This is the reason for the cross hairs locating the central point

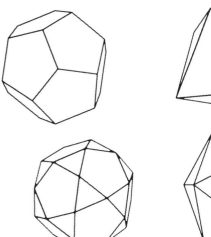
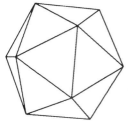

55

Square dance

At right is a chart showing a complete and comprehensive set of rotations of a cube through 180 degrees. Using exactly the same rules, we can rotate any object we wish into any position possible.

This can really help us visualize exactly what it is we are trying to achieve. Refer back to this set of images any time you have dificulty picturing what your object should look like from the angle you've tried to draw it. In other words, picture it placed inside the cube.

If you take a ruler you can observe the rules discussed earlier concerning orbits and their extensions. The reason they are excluded from this drawing is to show as clearly as possible the rotation, without the distracting clutter their inclusion would cause.

Each of the first four rows, on the opposite page, contain a variation of geometric based form. These objects have been rotated inside a cube. The first four have been rotated on a vertical axis across the page, viewed from ever-increasing angles along the horizon.

The other nine have been rotated using a horizontal axis, which has been rotated through 90 degrees.

The more we practice this, the quicker we will start to see any rotated object quickly in our mind's eye. For the Manga artist, the cube idea is just a means to an end, a tool that will help us bridge the gap between what we want to draw and the way things are in reality.

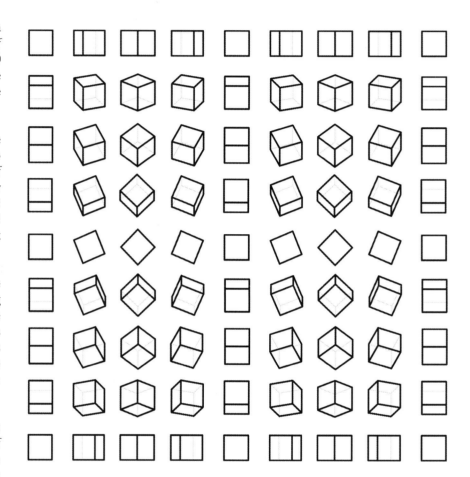

Once we've acheived this, we will be able to draw most things freehand. We'll have a working three-dimensional framework inside our minds, which should be able to automatically plot paths, trajectories, etc, and make them look right.

What stops us getting this stuff right? It's nothing more than a lack of the specialist information that is every artist's duty to learn. Without it, we shy away from the difficult stuff, or worse, draw something containing little or no understanding of

structure. The result is weak, unconvincing artwork.

But through practice, practice, practice, all of this information becomes second nature and we will be free to draw absolutely anything we like.

The above shows only the rotation in two directions. For a completely comprehensive rotation we would have to be working on a three-dimensional surface. i.e. a cube of cubes. If you need a challenge, try drawing that.

Geometric breakdown

Here is something far more Manga that demonstrates the theory and practice of the previous pages. On the facing page, there are two drawings. One is a representation of the drawing, the other is the drawing itself.

The top image is a geometric breakdown of the major components of the finished image. Everything has been reduced to its simplest geometric shape.

This shows us:

- the composition of the image, uncluttered by detail.
- that anything at all can be broken down into much simpler forms.
- that everything else is just superficial detail.

The superficial detail tends to be the thing that first excites a lot of people about Manga. The level of detail, the way the hair is drawn, clothes, lighting, robotic wiring, etc. But none of this would count for anything if what underpins the surface is not structurally sound.

To use an analogy with building construction: what's the point in building a beautiful palace if the foundations are lousy?

By blocking out our drawings first in basic geometric shapes, we can be totally sure that every element of the image hangs together before commiting huge amounts of time to the detail. Blocking out should take about 10% of the time the detail does.

The top image shows the breakdown in rather cold, lifeless shapes. It's been done like that purely to show the idea as clearly as possible. It is extremely unlikely we would ever draw our breakdowns with such geometric accuracy. When our drawing is fluid and really working we tend to bend, stretch and generally exaggerate the rules in order to breathe more life and expression into drawings. The robots are another example of geometry drawn without a ruler, which gives the lines a spontaneity.

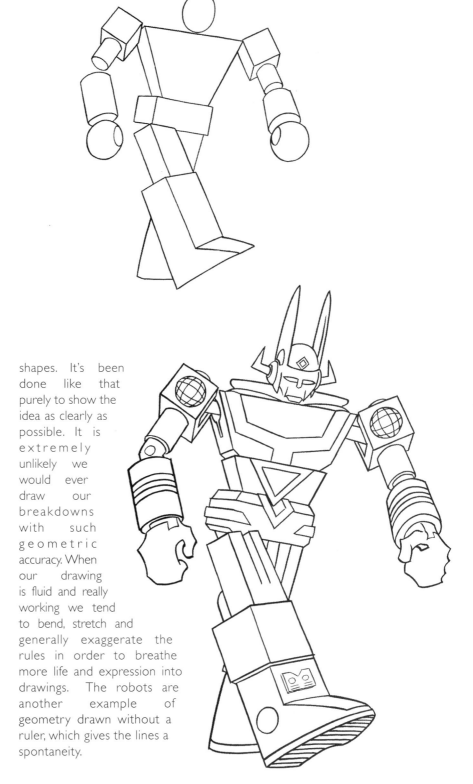

Grid it down

The grid is another handy tool for getting us out of trouble when we need to draw a complex view of an object.

Essentially, the grid is there to help break any image down into more manageable parts. With any change to the grid made, make the equivalent change to the image. It's all about containment and simplification.

On the facing page are several drawings which utilize this tool.

Figure A is a straight grid and copy; useful when something has to be totally accurate.

Figure B shows the result of "bulging" the grid. Notice how parts of the character are stretched and other parts shrunk. This is acheived quite simply by using the grid's exact guidelines.

Figure C skews the character at an eccentric angle, but again, if we follow the grid's guides, this is easily acheived.

As a general rule, the more complex the image you are gridding, the more lines your grid should have. Insufficient lines will lead to guesswork, which should be avoided at all costs.

In observational drawing, art classes often teach the cutting of a rectangle proportionate to the canvas out of card. Through this we concentrate on our composition.

A fine tuning of this method involves making a frame with thin parallel wires evenly spaced, perpendicular to the frame's edge. This hugely increases the ease with which we can map the composition. This works for both 2D and 3D, i.e. either a picture from a magazine or actual still life drawing.

Once mapped, an image can be described in numbers and/or letters. For example, it's easier to find Kingswood Avenue on a street plan if you know it exists in square 5A.

In essence, a digital camera maps an image on a grid, albeit at the most minute level. The space trapped between each point is called a pixel. Each pixel is given a value according to intensity and color. The computer can then interpret this abstracted information and display it.

This is how powerful grids can be. They are at the very heart of the huge majority of digital images we see.

In the early days of digital photography, there was a backlash by traditional photographers against the obvious pixellation that digital images displayed. Ironically, now that the technology is capable of matching the resolution of traditional film, there is a big movement celebrating the chunky delights of low-resolution images.

PIXEL ART

The crude type of graphics that were the best that early computer games could manage have now been revived as an art form in themselves. Known as Isometric Pixel Art, this form is based on the kind of 30 degree projections discussed earlier in the chapter.

For a fine, Manga-inspired example of this burgeoning art form, visit Gary Lucken's site: www.armyoftrolls.co.uk

For a forum on the subject, check out: http://pixelation.swoo.net

The backdrops used in theater are often produced using grids. The backdrop is initially drawn on a small scale, gridded and then scaled up by as much as a factor of 50, allowing the artist to reproduce a perfectly scaled copy.

Should you be seized with a desire to take one of your Manga characters and paint a 50ft version on a local building, this is exactly the method to use to achieve this.

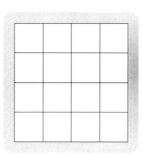

One of the best uses of grids is in the study of perspective. The perpendicular lines of the grid provide the perfect backdrop against which to study the effects and having these absolute lines cuts out guesswork and in doing so can save us a great deal of time.

fig. a   fig. b   fig. c

The point of perspective

The elements of perspective were dealt with in some detail in *Learn to Draw Manga – a Step-by-Step Guide*. But a brief overview of one, two, three and four-point perspective would be appropriate before moving on to the themes addressed in this book. Here goes:

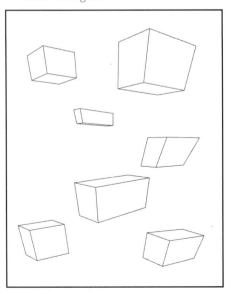

One-point perspective:
The most dramatic form, as all horizontal lines lead towards one single vanishing point. All objects are effectively viewed "head-on." All vertical lines are parallel.

Two-point perspective:
Instead of being viewed "head-on," we view the objects at an angle. This necessitates two vanishing points on the horizon, one for each horizontal plane. All vertical lines are parallel.

Three-point perspective:
This approach introduces a vertical vanishing point. What this means is objects don't just get smaller as they get nearer the horizon. They also get smaller as they move downward, towards an imaginary point at the center of the earth.

Four-point perspective:
Two horizontal vanishing points. Two vertical vanishing points. Used in "trick" images, this approach shows us what we could see if our field of vision was expanded to see both up and down simultaneously. This necessitates using a curved vertical line to imitate the gradual change from "up" to "down."

Perspective is a combination of both geometry and perception. What we see depends on where we are positioned, as well as what the object's form actually is. Although we use straight lines to work out perspective, in reality there is no such thing as a truly straight line.

Two factors make this so: one is the curvature of the earth, the other is

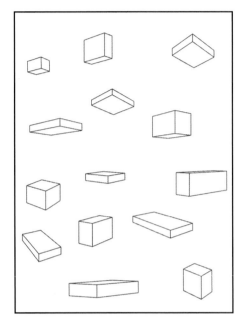

the construction of our eyes.

With the exception of four-point perspective, for reasons just explained, a straight line is almost always perfectly acceptable.

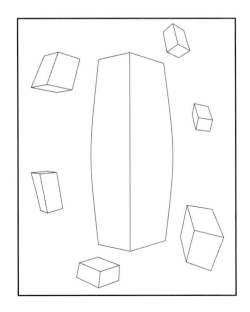

The above drawing is an exercise showing the use of a plumbline. This is a vertical line which is always 90 degrees to the horizon line. Together they form what we'll call "cross-hairs."

The cross-hairs in the image above show where our center of vision is located. With reference to this a ruler was taken and the above study was made. In this example, none of the horizontal perspective lines are coming straight at us. In fact, the horizontal vanishing points are not even inside the picture frame at all.

This is a good way of avoiding images looking too obvious and can help give a more naturlistic feel.

The plumbline in this case consisted of a length of string with an eraser attached to one end. This provided a constant 90 degree reference point, against which the interior's perspective could be compared.

A doorway viewed head-on is an excellent example of extreme perspective. If you want to gain a better understanding, make a study of a door drawn from this viewpoint. Better still, make several studies at different eye levels.

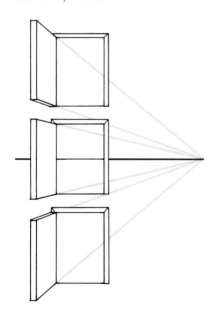

With paper frame

The frame device is an ideal tool for studying perspective. It restricts the view, creating absolute boundaries to vision. Undistracted, we can then compare what is in our field of vision with the frame's vertical lines. The images below left show what the Eyeball Kid is seeing when he uses this device. The diagrams below right show him holding the frame and the journey of selected paths of light traveling to him through the frame.

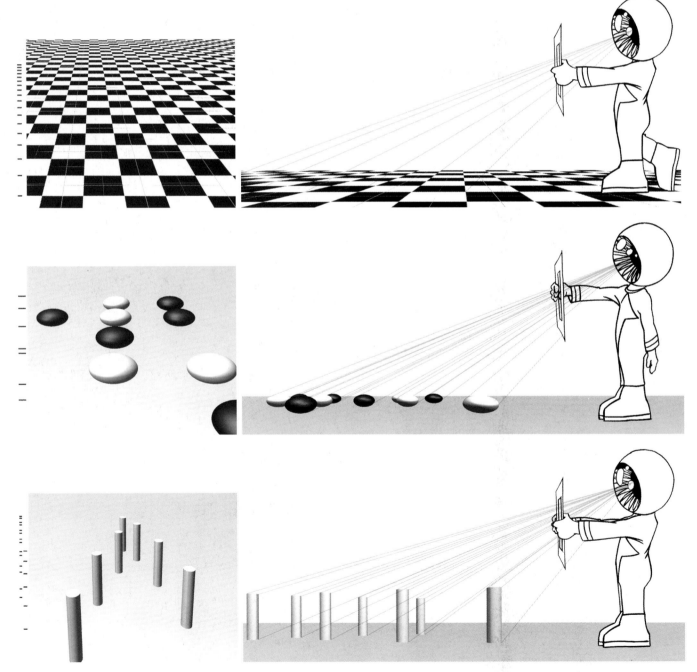

Another important phenomenon to note is the way objects change shape as they move towards or away from us.

At top left the Eyeball Kid is looking at a flat chequered surface. Notice how the shapes become increasingly less square as they move away.

At middle left we can see the same phenomenon, but this time it occurs with a three-dimensional shape. The closer an object below the horizon line moves towards our feet, the more we are looking down on it. Conversely the nearer the horizon, the more of a side view we get.

This is even clearer at bottom left. All of the posts are exactly the same shape and size. But our perception of them alters as they recede into the distance.

The lines in the right-hand drawings show what it happening here. You can clearly see how the angle changes, altering our viewpoint. This is clearly three-point perspective: one vertical vanishing point and two horizontal ones.

You'll notice some small lines at the margins of the left-hand images on page 64. If we imagine the area outside of the images represent our frame, these small marks are the points at which the reflected light of the objects pass through the frame on their way to our eyes. Check these against the gray angled lines in the right-hand images. You'll find they match exactly.

Not all the objects depicted make it

through the frame, which is why they are not visible in the left-hand images. Look at the objects nearest to the Eyeball Kid's feet to see what we mean.

The image above demonstrates that these principles don't only apply to areas beneath the horizon line. We can employ exactly the same ideas when dealing with walls and ceilings.

This corridor is constructed using simple one-point perspective, a device often used in Manga to depict ducts, lifts and tunnels. But the objects on the walls do not have parallel lines, i.e. their angles increase as they get closer to us. This means the image above has to be three-point perspective, even if it is not immediately obvious.

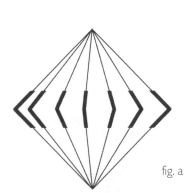

fig. a

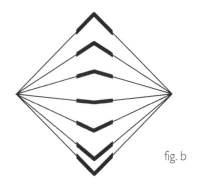

fig. b

Where's the viewer?

The images above show the same angle viewed first horizontally and then vertically. We know the angle is exactly the same, as it has the same vanishing point. However, our position in relation to it has a massive impact.

If the archer in the above picture keeps the bow and arrow drawn back but then aims in an arc, towards and away from us, we see exactly the same phenomenon as in fig. a.

If he were to keep it pulled back but rotated his wrist to hold the bow in a flat position, then aimed up and down, we would get the pattern shown in fig. b.

Below shows the Eyeball Kid contemplating a still life scene. To the right is the scene as it reaches his cornea. Not only is it bulged out, it's also upside down. This is how images, as light, actually reach our eyes.

At bottom right is a simple diagram showing what's actually happening to the visual information as it travels through our iris towards the back of the eye, known as the macula. On the previous pages we saw how the light traveled toward the eye. As light travels only in straight lines, it passes through the iris and is projected onto the back of the eye upside-down. Because this area is curved the image has the depicted bulge shape. The brain then interprets this information into something more practical, i.e. what we actually percieve.

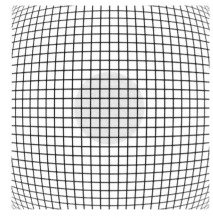

Above is a representation of the back of our eye. The curved grid pattern is the macula — the back wall of the eye. The dark spot at the center depicts the fovea, a small area at the center of the macula which has the highest concentration of sensors. These sensors are responsible for our very sharpest vision and are it's central point of focus.

So what happens to our vision as we move away from this central point? With less high-definition sensors, we have less clarity. The fovea is the only point in the macula unobstructed by blood vessels or nerve endings.

As we move outwards from the fovea we come into the part of the macula far more concerned with detecting movement in what is called our peripheral vision. Between these two different functions we have an eye which combines a general motion detection with sharp focus.

There are two straight lines on the grid above: the central horizontal and the central vertical. The point at which these converge is right in the middle of our fovea, the point of sharpest clarity. This explains much

of the phenomena which we have discussed in this chapter. It's no coincidence that where these two lines cross, they form right angles, the basis for a cube.

Why is this important for a Manga artist? What we are doing when we create an image on paper is an attempt to imitate what the viewer's eye experiences when it beholds the real world. The more we understand about this process, the

better equipped we are to play around with the stuff of perception. And by doing this we can create not only believable worlds, but push our images beyond the normal field of vision.

The large image above does exactly that. We can't normally see in all four directions at once, but through an understanding of the process we can create an image that shows what it would look like if we could.

Facing page:

At top, we've taken the rules of perspective, but dramatically curved all the lines. Extended further they would actually curve in on themselves, but what this view does is hugely intensify the curve on the macula, creating a bizarre, but believable space.

Below left is an example of a common practice in Manga. There is no background as such. Instead we have three sets of speed lines giving a sense not only of motion but also of space. This is made possible by an understanding of the rules of perspective. Without this, the lines would probably conflict and confuse the viewer.

Right: the eye sends signals to the brain via the optic nerve as a series of pulses. These are not entirely dissimilar to the frames of a movie. If we reduced the "frame rate" of these pulses, this would inhibit the brain's ability to interpret and decipher what we see, resulting in an image similar to the one here.

Each section of the picture works by itself, but when we attempt to match them up, we are missing the interpretive parts, causing a mismatch between the individual "frames."

All of the images continued in the last few pages are essentially having fun with reality. But they also help enrich our understanding of what's possible. This in turn adds to our ability to make the worlds we draw both dramatic and believable.

Head for heights

The information about approaches to making our drawings believable can be tested by drawing a massive cityscape, pulling in as much of our knowledge about perspective as possible. We'll throw in a couple of characters for human interest and see if we can't induce a bit of vertigo at the same time.

It all starts with the planning of course. Horizon line, horizontal vanishing points, vertical vanishing points. Then we begin blocking out, calculating what looks best where and generally feeling our way into the cityscape.

As we build it up, we should start to get a feeling of "being in the landscape." If we can't make ourselves believe we're there, we'll have little chance of convincing anyone else.

One novel feature of this landscape is the "detour" in the central street below. This effectively throws all the vanishing points past a certain line off-kilter, producing a far less predictable and more dense urban environment. The viewer is also placed near to the two girls (see page 72) but has no clue as to what, if anything, is supporting the viewer.

You'll probably notice the almost complete absence of any areas of pure black. This is because the image has been drawn ultimately to be rendered in full color. For the final result see the color section.

The drawing here shows how we begin. The horizon line is established, but at a tilted angle for added drama and giddiness. We'll then put a few

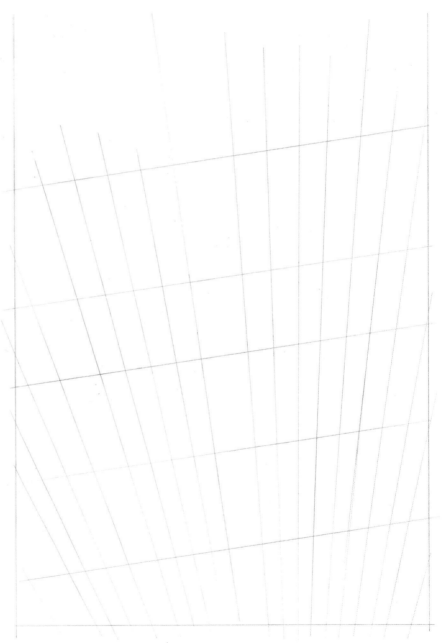

more rough guidelines down the page parallel with the horizon.

Next establish the vertical vanishing point. This is clearly way off the page, so an extra long ruler or straight edge is useful here. Make sure the

central vertical line is more or less in the center of the page. This is always the line perpendicular to the horizon. Either side of this, add several more vertical guidelines. Now we're ready to add some horizontals.

In this picture, we've established several horizontal lines leading to a central vanishing point.

Next comes the tricky part. We now have to use our imaginations to "see" possibilities on the page. For many people, this can prove to be the toughest part of the job. Learning technical skills is one thing, but they alone will only carry us so far. If you're finding it difficult to visualize buildings etc, it's a good idea to get some reference which may spark off some ideas about where to place what.

Don't become bogged down in detail at this stage. We're still at the planning part of the drawing. No detail should be added until all of the major structures are established. In the drawing at left, we're a fair way to establishing the buildings occupying the immediate field of vision.

In order to give the viewer a plunging sense of vertigo, we've left the area immediately in front of their feet void of any buildings or other structures. This gives a palpable feeling of depth and shows off the extreme use of perspective well. There's no handrail for the viewer to cling to and they don't even know what they are standing on.

What will also help put the viewer in the picture is some fellow humans. This is particularly important for establishing scale. The human eye will naturally and unconciously measure things against the scale of the human body. Putting two characters on the opposite rooftop makes a big difference. Just compare the picture at left with the one overleaf.

The central, cylindrical building is loosely based on a tower in Tokyo. It's a good shape to break things up a little, as too many square buildings can make for a dull landscape. The more variety we can pack into our landscape, the more depth it will ultimately seem to have. If the viewer can look at a picture like this and immediately see and understand everything, it simply won't hold their attention. The human mind is naturally curious. We should aim to keep this curiosity burning as much as possible.

Now for ink

At right is the drawing with about 95% of the work in place. It has the right balance of detail and simplicity and achieves what it set out to do. There are just a few little nips and tucks to perform before we get the ink bottle out.

But first let's see what's been added since the previous page.

Probably the most important feature is the sudden bend in the street plan. As mentioned on page 70, this is a device not only to add more depth and interest to the image, but also to provide a fresh challenge for ourselves. It really would be a bit dull if every building simply went to the same vanishing point. It would also be quite unrealistic. Although most modern cities are built on a grid-type street plan, these kind of sudden deviations are almost always present.

Having our girl characters looking down into the several hundred feet drop is another way to draw the viewer in, the girl at the back has got a pretty tight grip on those railings.

Towers, arials, etc, are a good way of breaking up a skyline. They form part of the landscape of all modern cities. Whether a space needle or an old radio mast, these details help provide texture.

Rooftops are always worth studying. What's on the rooftops depends enormously on what city we are in. Water towers tend to dominate the rooftops of New York, while air conditioning ducts, solar panels, helipads, etc, may be more prominent in other cities. A cityscape

with bare rooftops is never going to be believable, so why not download a few images for reference?

Opposite is the finished ink drawing. As explained, there are no heavy black areas in the picture at the moment as ultimately it will be taken into color for the final image. With

this in mind, all of the lines are tight, and without gaps. This is essential to avoid spending hours on fix-ups in a graphics program, in order to make sure the individual areas hold color.

If your planning is good, there's no reason at all you shouldn't produce even more involved images.

Matchstalks

Below is a sample of a huge number of variations on these ideas. But they all work on the same principle by using the workings of the eye to convince the viewer that they are not looking at a flat piece of paper.

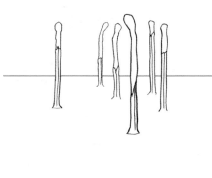

Here is a simple exercise which demonstrates other ways to enhance the feeling of distance between objects.

When we have no obvious perpective lines we have to look to other things to help us out. They are: scale, detail and line strength.

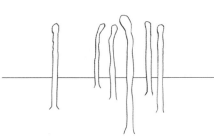

Scale is probably the most obvious. Provided the brain can tell that the images are consistent in size, a reduction in scale will mean the objects are receding.

Detail diminishes the further it is from the eye, provided focus is consistent. One way to remove detail is by blurring, either by using soluble ink or on a computer. This is not always practical though as it may not be suitable for the printing process.

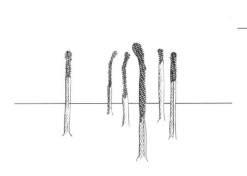

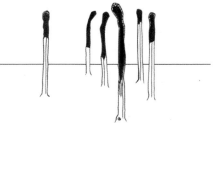

Line strength is an excellent way to convey a feeling of depth, although it is also the most artificial. In reality, objects are not made of outlines. This however does not prevent us from drawing on the eye's and brain's natural interpretation of things.

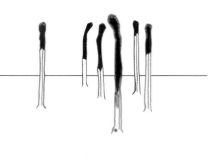

The above picture should demonstrate the usefulness of the exercise. The better we are at drawing matchstalks convincingly, the better our drawings of trees, lamposts, street signs, etc, will be.

The most immediately obvious techniques in the above image are the use of line weight and detail. In the foreground the bark of the trees approaches pure black. The outlines are also much heavier. The detail on the ground is also reduced to almost nothing as the scene moves towards the horizon.

Another important factor here is the consistency with which all the trees are rendered. The same technique is employed throughout, with diminishing strength as the trees are further away. This immediately helps the eye make sense of what it is seeing. A variety of treatments would add needless complication to the scene and ultimately detract from its readability, which is of the greatest importance. We want to put the viewer into the scene as quickly as possible. This isn't possible if part or all of the image first has to be decoded.

One last obvious feature is the use of heavy shadow. This serves several purposes. Like the shadow on the bark, it becomes less heavy as it recedes. It also has its own perspective, adding to the depth of the picture. Lastly, it gives us some information about the time of day. Long shadows like these are only cast in the early morning or towards dusk.

Let there be light

What is light?

Without light, objects have no visible form. Our eyes and brains automatically translate the effect light has on an object to give us a sense of its form.

In the above image, we see a single light source shining on a cylinder from the side. The right-hand side shows complete saturation of the object's surface by the light. Conversely, the left side demonstrates a complete absence of light. This is due to the object itself blocking the further progress of the light particles, either through absorbtion or reflection. The graduation from light to dark is indicative of how the surface plane gradually turns from the light until it is beyond its influence.

A shadow therefore is an area where light has failed to penetrate. We are used to thinking of shadows being cast, but it can help to think of it the

other way around. Think for a moment of complete darkness being the normal state of affairs, and light as something that intrudes upon this.

All light is directional in that it has a source from which it proceeds. It does so in a straight line until it makes

contact with a surface, illuminating that surface and anything else that falls within its reach. In the case of a spotlight, this reach is very restricted, producing a cone-shaped beam of light. This is due to most of the light source being contained within the spotlight's casing. The sun on the other

hand is omni-directional, radiating light across 360 degrees. Although the sun's light is still directional, it has a huge coverage of half a planet at any one time. This means there is also a great deal of reflected light to consider when drawing daylight exteriors.

The seven sets of posts at left demonstrates the shadows cast as the sun moves through the sky in the course of a day. A practical use of this is the sundial.

Above is a composite of all seven sets, showing the extents of the shadows from dawn to dusk. Obviously, the shadows move smoothly and imperceptibly throughout the day.

The image at the bottom of the page is a representation of moonlight. The shadows themselves are no darker than in the daytime, but there is very little contrast as all of the light is reflected. At night, the moon acts as a weak mirror to the sun. All the light we receive at night is what has managed to reach us after reflecting from the moon's surface.

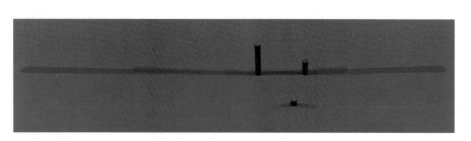

Here are a number of single and multiple source examples. The first image shows light interacting with a regular cube. The lines show how the light flow is interrupted by the extent of the cube's form, casting a pentagonal shadow as it does so.

Provided we know where the source of the light is located, we can easily work out the extent of any shadow cast using this method.

How about multiple light sources? The same rules apply but the difficulty arises when the results overlay each other. Figure A shows the result of eight equal powered light sources arranged evenly around our cube. There are five different levels of interaction here, varying in darkness from adjacent to the object outward. The closer the shadow is to the object, the more interaction there is.

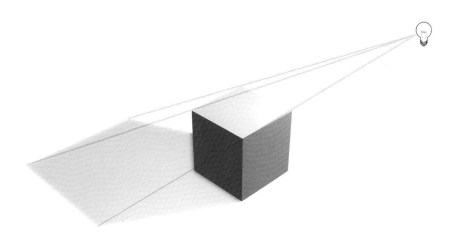

Figure B shows what happens when the light intensity is so powerful that any shadow around the object is obliterated by reflected light. There is an optimum amount of light to produce a good balance of contrast between object and shadow. Figure B

goes way beyond this. Figures C and D have far more variation in their light sources, both in their placement and their intensity. This results in a far less predictable set of shadows being cast, with the widest possible range of shadow tones.

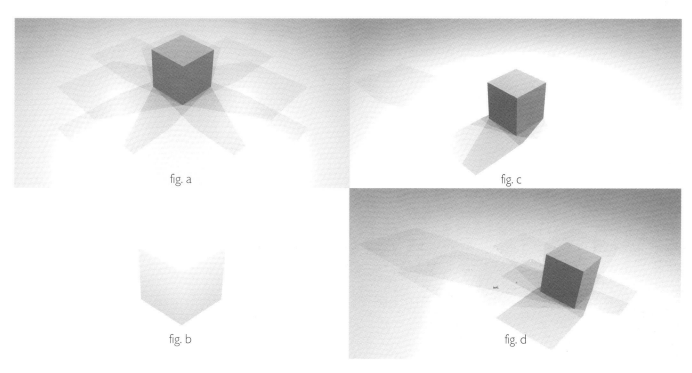

fig. a

fig. b

fig. c

fig. d

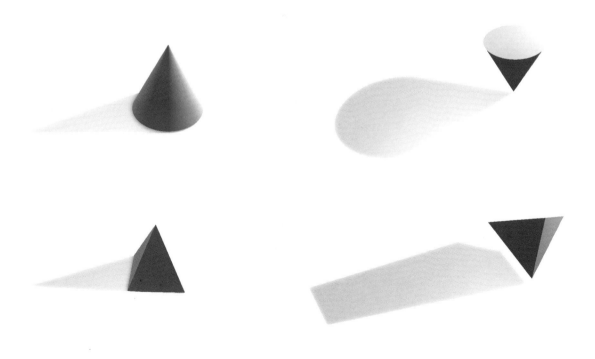

Here we see the shapes of shadows produced by other geometric shapes. If we can work out why these objects cast the shadows they do, we should be able to create accurate shadowing for any shape.

Using the same principles as on the previous page, try drawing the lines from the shadow, past the object and continue. The point where these lines meet should be the light source. If our lines don't join at the same point,

they have been miscalculated.

If an object is not making contact with its shadow this means there is a gap between the object and the surface the shadow is being cast upon.

The circle's shadows are reasonably obvious and could be guessed with confidence. Similarly, the cone and pyramid when upright are just as predictable. The more challenging shadows are the ones cast by the

tilted, upside-down objects. Could we accurately predict the shape of the shadow cast in the bottom right image? With practice and experience we get used to the way light behaves, making it increasingly easier to "see" and quickly work out such shapes.

Shadows tell us not only about the form of the object, but also the light source and the relationship between the object and the surface of its shadow.

Geometric shapes are all very well, but what about the very stuff of Manga, the human face?

The human face is a complex structure, but fortunately it's one we already know very well so it shouldn't be too difficult to work out how light behaves when it hits it.

From top to bottom we have the effect of single-source lighting moving from directly above the head through being shone directly at the face down to being lit from under

atmospheric effect. When done to a less extreme degree, this uplighting can be excellent in depicting evil characters.

When lighting the face from the side, we have to consider the parts that face away from the light. But how much shadow is cast is dependent on two factors: how far the feature protrudes from the face, and how large an area it occupies. For instance, the end of the nose protrudes more than the upper lip, but the upper lip and chin

the chin. From left to right follows the same progression, but with radically different results.

The top image has the effect of bringing out the shape of the skull. The eyes disappear, often completely and the cheekbones stand out in stark relief. This makes it a great way to light gothic horror stories.

The bottom is almost an inversion of the top one, with the light picking out the chin, mouth, tip of the nose, bottom eyelids, eyes and lower eyebrows. This too has a very

area is wider. At a certain, critical point, the shadows all coalesce, plunging one side of the face into sillhouette.

The hair shine follows the light source as it moves around the head. In the bottom image, the light never reaches the hair, explaining its solid blacks.

To really get to grips with this, use a powerful torch and a mirror. Move the torch around your own face and observe the results, taking notes for later use.

There's more

Real life situations teach us how wild and unpredictable light can be, especially where the human body is concerned.

With the advent of cameras in phones, it's possible to obtain instant references, but more important than the camera you use is getting the lighting right. Work out in advance what it is you are trying to achieve, then use the lighting to pick out the surface of your subject.

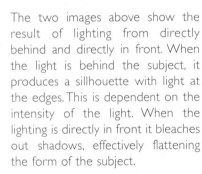

The two images above show the result of lighting from directly behind and directly in front. When the light is behind the subject, it produces a sillhouette with light at the edges. This is dependent on the intensity of the light. When the lighting is directly in front it bleaches out shadows, effectively flattening the form of the subject.

The images on page 79 are idealized and simplified and use only pure blacks to achieve their effect. Any grays have been made either black or white to get at the pure essence of the lighting.

Using your own reference is extremely important. This is the way we make our own discoveries and bring something new to the field. Looking at the work of other Manga artists can be inspiring and help our

understanding. If Manga artists looked only at each other's work the creative well would quickly become dry and make Manga a spent force. As it is, the very best artists are continually bringing new visual approaches keeping it the vibrant, ever-evolving form it currently is.

For some prime examples of Manga-kas using the techniques in this section, check out the works of Kia Asimiya (*Silent Mobius*), Yuzou Takada (*3x3Eyes*), Tsutomu Nihei (*Blame*) and Maki Kusumoto (*Kiss xxx*). All of these artists have a deep understanding of light and perspective and bring their own ideas and approaches to the medium.

For a more comprehensive list of top Manga artists, check out the glossary at the back of this book.

LIGHT STUDIES

In the first chapter we looked at some sketches and studies done in inkpen, using various weights to make useful visual notes.

But ink is not necessarily the best medium for making light studies. Other media such as charcoal or acrylics can give us a far more in-depth result.

The image to our right was made using charcoal. But instead of using black on white to depict shadow, the paper was first smothered in charcoal. A putty eraser was then used to sculpt out the light of the figure.

The two images at the bottom were done in roughly 15 minutes each. By using acrylic, it was possible to apply and mix the tonal values right there on the canvas. A wide, flat brush was used for maximum variety of stroke.

Theory is one thing, but practice is something else altogether. It is the only thing that is guaranteed to improve our work. Even the days when we feel we have learned nothing from practice are not wasted. It is almost impossible to set yourself a drawing task and not get something worthwhile from the exercise, no matter how lousy you may think the results are.

There are many potential pitfalls along the way, the first of which is the feeling that we need to be doing something that impresses: either ourselves or more often, other people. Sure, rotating a cube or undertaking a matchstalk study is unlikely to draw major accolades, but, if we are determined to be not just a superficially talented artist, but one that actually knows what's what, we need to become keen observers of everything and anything.

What is ultimately impressive about Manga is how every aspect of the form is understood by so many artists. Too many Western comic book artists seem to feel that it's enough to master only one aspect of their craft, usually the superficially impressive stuff. But many of the great Manga artists excel in most (and sometimes even all) aspects of their craft.

Have a good look at the work of Masamune Shirow. He is the author/artist of *Appleseed* and *Ghost in the Shell*. There is not a single aspect of his art of which he does not have an incredibly strong grasp. Perspectve, figure drawing, architecture, lighting — it's all in there in spades. This is what we are aspiring to: total command of the worlds we create and everything that populates them.

SECTION 0.3

Going digital

At some point we all want to reproduce our Manga. With current technology, this is easier than ever. Whether we want to produce a short run of 100 issues, assembled and printed using a home computer, or a run of several thousand employing the service of professional printers, once the drawing is completed our images will have to become digital.

Assuming we're not possessed by a perverse urge to reproduce our beautiful artwork as badly as possible, then some small considerations can help ensure a good result. For example washing our hands before we begin to draw. This not only results in a smoother more fluid line because of reduced friction, but any tiny amounts of sweat, pencil lead, etc that would normally mark the paper will also be taken out of the equation. We may not be able to see this, but a scanner can. Especially because this residue can be a haven for all sorts of gathering dust and muck.

How do we obtain the optimum result from our scanner? Once scanned what is the best format to store the image? Is there anything we can do to improve or correct the original piece? Much can be done with the aid of a graphics program. Gimp, Corel Draw, Photoshop and Fireworks, to name a few. But the better the initial drawing the better the scan and therefore the easier it is to get a great end result.

Although this chapter is heavily computer-oriented we'll be looking at the process in terms of the principles. Understanding what's happening can facilitate the discovery of your own methods. If you are already skilled with graphics programs and computers then perhaps a different approach may increase your understanding and expertise. It is the little detail that make the difference between good and amazing.

File types

There are two main types of digital graphic images:

RASTER IMAGES

These are pixel-based which means the image is broken down first by the scanner and then arranged into a grid made of tiny squares. Because this is done pixel-by-pixel and may involve millions of them, these types of files tend to be very large when uncompressed.

File types vary depending on the type and amount of compression they use. JPEG files are highly compressed, which is fine for viewing on a monitor, but would look lousy if used on the printed page. JPEGs are the dominant file type found on the internet.

TIFF files are far less compressed, and often not compressed at all. They correspondingly have a much greater resolution and are far more suitable for print. The images that you see in this book are all uncompressed TIFF format.

Other Raster file types include:

GIF which are again, ideal for flat color for the internet but not much else.

BMP or bitmap, which use only black or white pixels. Much more on this type later.

Knowing what is going on inside your processor when you use say, a distort filter, means you can make far more informed decisions about your images. Being certain that the pixels we need to select with the color range tool are around the value of 65 allows us to judge exactly just what gets selected and subsequently what gets altered.

VECTOR BASED IMAGES

These work on math rather than pixels. The advantage of this is that resolution is not an issue. The image can be displayed any size from near invisible to the size of a billboard and not lose any definition. Points are plotted and then stored as a set of instructions by the computer. These instructions are then used to recreate the image anywhere at any size.

Vector programs such as Flash are particularly popular with internet designers due to their small file size. This could mean as little as one-100th of the size of the equivalent Raster image. The title text on this book's cover was initially created using vector graphics and then converted to Raster when the image was finalized. With Manga, text is the most likely application of Vector graphics, unless you plan to make online Manga.

Scanning and printing

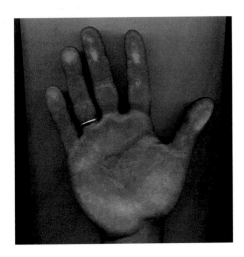

Getting images into the computer is straightforward enough, but what about the specifics?

All scanners have software to communicate with graphics programs. It's here that we make the important decisions about the quality and size of the scan. The single most important factor we have control over is the dpi. This stands for dots per inch, although it can be set per centimeter if you prefer. By dots, we mean pixels. In plain terms, this means that at 300 dpi, one inch of the image above will be broken down into 300 separate pixels per line. At 600 dpi it's obviously twice that number. This has a dramatic effect on the resolution of our images. The higher the dpi the truer to the original image the scan will be.

What's best for scanning Manga? 300 dpi is the minimum. This will produce a pretty reasonable reproduction of the artwork. But at 600 dpi the image will be sharper and more accurate. So why not scan everything with as high a dpi as possible? The first reason is file size. As we increase the resolution of our scans, the file size

increases exponentially. With big scans, this can result in a file so colossal our computer will have a tough time just moving it around the screen, let alone performing highly involved filter operations.

The second reason is concerned with interpolation. Above a certain dpi, depending on the quality of our scanner, the machine stops actually creating new pixels and starts making it up. By this I mean rather than recreate the image faithfully with pixels, it *interpolates* or fills in the gaps that the physical limits of the scanner's hardware prevent it from creating. With the majority of domestic scanners, 600 dpi is the hardware limit. Scanning much above this on such machines achieves little or nothing.

The same thing happens if we increase the dpi using our graphics programs. A 300 dpi image increased to 1200 dpi achieves nothing, except to make a bigger version of exactly the same thing.

This should make it clear that the scanning stage is paramount to getting good results. You can reduce a 600 dpi image to 300 dpi once you're happy with it, but doing things in the other direction is pointless.

The majority of the images in this book were scanned at 400 dpi, then reduced in size by as much as 70 percent. This gives a tight, crisp definition. For the black and white pages, no higher dpi would be needed. The color section is printed on much higher definition stock and so benefits from additional resolution of up to 600 dpi.

There are two types of color file you are likely to need to know about.

CMYK – Cyan (C), Magenta (M), Yellow (Y) and Black (K). These refer to the physical print colors used to produce the color artwork. This is the print industry standard and the color type you would be expected to present to a professional. It will look different on your display and may need quite a bit of adjustment if you've scanned it in as an RGB.

RGB – Red, Green and Blue. These refer not to the print colors, but instead to the color guns of an old style "tube" or tv/monitor. Accordingly, when we adjust the color values of an RGB file, we are changing the way the file is displayed, not the way the file is printed. RGB looks great on your screen, but is not necessarily an accurate picture of your output. More importantly, professional printers do not print from RGB. If you give an RGB file to a printer, it would probably be automatically converted to CMYK. The results would be a lot different to how it appeared on screen and probably much more drab.

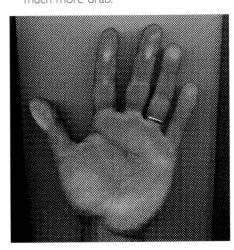

The good the bad and the smudgy

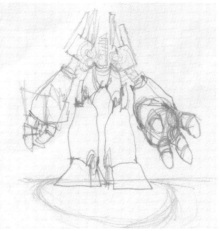
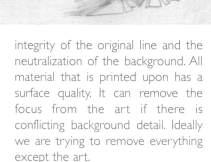

Naturally we want our drawings to look amazing but what can we do to guarantee this?

Above are three freshly scanned drawings. All are quite beautiful but the quality of each is remarkably different. The primary reason for this is the materials used: The first in the sequence was drawn on very smooth white paper, a type known as Bristol Board. The other two were drawn on good quality art paper. It has a slightly textured surface and is not pure white. The scanner has noticed this and proudly reproduced every tiny detail. The second material difference is the pencil weight. The first is made with an "F" pencil, a clean hard line that is difficult to smudge. The other two drawings are done with a much softer pencil.

The last two are much more expressive and obviously created as pieces of stand-alone artwork. The first is a working drawing and therefore less attention has been given to surface detail. Another reason why the drawing is cleaner and will be easier to make more so.

Why are we looking at pencil drawings when most Manga comics are drawn in ink? Because there is less contrast, pencil is much harder to clean up than ink.

The two diagrams below show a hard pencil line, a soft pencil line and a brush stroke on – both smooth and rough – paper. Also we can observe a top half and bottom half to each. Two things to remember when approaching clean up work: It is important to try and maintain the

integrity of the original line and the neutralization of the background. All material that is printed upon has a surface quality. It can remove the focus from the art if there is conflicting background detail. Ideally we are trying to remove everything except the art.

As we see in the lower halves of each diagram, in direct comparison to the upper half, the line has lost the quality of the original due to over-cleaning.

The big easy

Above is the unadulterated scan. So what is the first thing we should do to the image now that we have it open in our preferred graphics program? Neutralize the background.

As Photoshop seems currently the most widely used graphics program we will descibe this in their terms. However as the tools required are the most basic they should be included in all but the most unsophisticated software.

We could use the *Contrast* tool – nestled in the *Images* dropdown menu/adjustments. This allows us to increase the difference between the dark and light parts of the image and, on a separate slider, increase the complete tone of the image as a whole. Unfortunately for this delicate work it is rather a clumsy tool. The contrast slider tries to do two things at the same time; it increases lightness and darkness simultaneously. The Brightness slider also works universaly with both.

What we need to be able to do is adjust each tone individually. For this

we look to the *Levels* control in the same dropdown subsection. The image to our right has been divided into thirds and each third has been adjusted individually. The first third has had a dramatic increase in black tone. The middle third has a mixture of both tones and the final third an increase of the white. Obviously, this has been done to extremes in order to demonstrate the effects. The principle is very simple: the gradient bar below the image moves from black through to white with increments from 0 (pure black) through to 255 (pure white). Any given pixel in an image has a tonal value from 0 to 255. To increase the dark tone value slider to say 25 is to tell the computer that any pixel from 0 to 25 should now be treated as having the value 0 (pure black). It is the same when you decrease the value slider from the white end, but in reverse. So for example, if the paper is slightly off white, say with a value around 240, and the tonal value range of the pencil image is between 75 and 235, we can safely bring the white slider down to eliminate the background without any compromise to the pencil. Also, if we feel that the pencil line is too weak we can increase the position at which the black begins, with the effect of increasing pencil line tonal value. With a really clean image this is often all that needs to be done.

There are other options on this tool; a central

slider which allows you to bias the tonal balance of an image. Move it towards the white and the range between black and mid-gray will increase, whilst the range between mid-gray and white will decrease, or vise versa. This gives a subtle fine tuning to the balance of an image. Any random marks remaining can be removed with the paint brush tool set to white.

The bad

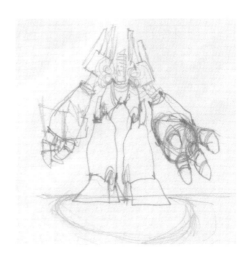

The above drawing has been made on rougher, less white paper. As with the previous page, it is the unadulterated scan. Adding to the problems of a non-white paper and soft pencil depth on the figure is a wide variation in the strength of the pencil line. This gives the pencil marks a range of tonal values – between about 40 and 240.

This in turn means that there is a smaller margin of adjustment before the actual drawing is effected. Below is an extreme division into thirds, demonstrating the dilemma. So what can be done to "free" the drawing from the gray background? After

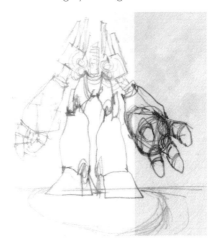

improving it as much as possible with the *Levels* method it is tackled using a different tool. In the *Select* drop down menu find the *Color Range* tool. Use the most sensitive setting for the color white, i.e. fuzziness=0. This results in what are known as "marching ants" around all the pure white pixels.

The diagram to the right is the result of inverting the selection so that everything that is not pure white is selected and then filled with a 50% gray. So with the white pixels selected, we expand our marching ants borders by one pixel and then contract by the same amount. The result is that all the two pixel wide grime is consumed whilst the rest of the image remains intact. We can feather the edge 0.5 of a pixel and fill the slightly increased area with white.

This can be repeated with a slightly higher tolerance on the *Color Range* sensitivity, which is described fuzziness. and then repeated and repeated. This will slowly encroach into the sludge. It should also be noted that the higher the dpi of the image the more flexibilty we have with pixel ajustments such as these. Scan big, but not stupidly so. Once the adjustments are finished, the image may be reduced to the size required.

There is a very good reason for working gradually. This method soon reaches the limit of its effectiveness and the

remaining sludge clots together. To continue could also damage the integrity of the pencil lines. Every image is different and it makes sense to vary the method to suit each situation. It's up to you to adapt each method to your needs.

Any remaining clots can be cleaned up with the brush tool. From the above sludge gray picture to the below final image shows just how effective this approach can be.

And the smudgy

The most difficult part in cleaning a drawing with this much gray area is deciding what is integral to the image as a whole.

Have another look at the charcoal sketch near the end of chapter two. There was no pure white or pure black, and the drawing goes right to the edge of the paper. With no background as such, the job becomes easier. Adjust the balance so that the image remains true to the original. Then reproduce it to the edge of the paper or place it within a frame.

The image above contains pencil lines with values similar to the background.

We need to remove the background, whilst keeping the pencils intact. At bottom left is a fast, but extreme solution. Although this results in a strong, easily reproducible image, the final result is quite some way from the original. Much of the subtlety of line has been destroyed with such a heavy-handed approach. One should only resort to such methods when time constraints provide little choice.

In the images on the right-hand side of the page we have followed the same routine as before. First, we adjust the levels, the black, the white and then tweak the balance. When we begin clean up, it's a good idea to keep open an example or two of the most successful adjustments for comparison.

Then follow the *color range* expand and contract / feather and fill method. This drawing required rather more hands-on retouching than normal. The cleaner an image is to begin with, the quicker and better it can be prepared. This is one area where the more time spent fixing an image the more likely we are to damage it. Besides, touch up work is dull and can quickly drain enthusiasm. Advances in print technology mean higher quality images, but there's a good reason most comic art is inked.

Easy ink

Cleaning up a tight ink drawing is a comparitive joy. Scanning the pencils is not necessary, but has been included for the sake of instruction. Understanding another artist's working method is often useful. A few artists go straight to ink, but most begin with a pencil version.

Following this is another unadulterated scan of the inked pencils. Physically erasing the pencils can often weaken the ink lines. With the advent of computers it is generally unnecessary. If they are particularly heavy they can be lightened gently with a putty rubber.

The third image in the sequence has only been adjusted with the levels panel, and the surrounding marks have practically vanished. The fourth image is the same, but with the black emphasized. This was simply done by selecting all white using the *Color Range* tool with zero fuzziness. This was inverted and filled with black. If we have good clean line, this selection and inversion can be used to strengthen or lighten an image's line, but for best results it is often best to slightly feather the selection before filling.

For example in a 400 dpi 12cm by 12cm image, the lines are too weak. Select all the blacks at maximum fuzziness, feather 0.5 pixels and fill with black. This will slightly increase the width and retain quality. If these lines really needed a boost we could expand the selection. But remember the more you alter the image the more likely it is to be damaged.

Continuing with the sequence to the

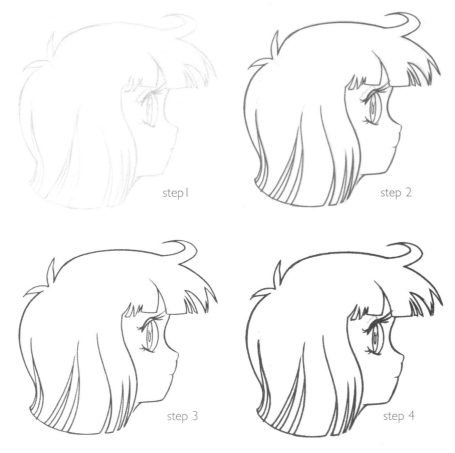

step 1

step 2

step 3

step 4

right: After adjusting the levels, all the black at maximum fuzziness was selected. Then the selection was expanded, feathered at 0.5 pixels, inverted and filled with white. This can be completed in less than a minute, along with a few minor corrections to the drawing, made with the brush tool. It would also be advisable to specifically level the ends of the hair and darken the eyelashes and pupil.

step 5

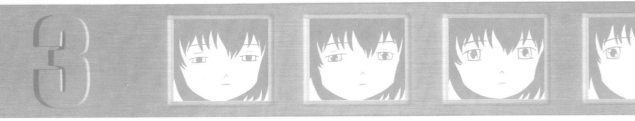

Deep down and dirty

The sequence of drawings at right follow as on the previous page. First off, we have the pencils, drawn on white smooth paper with an "H" pencil. Then we have the inked version of the same drawing, followed by an image where the levels have been altered. A small section of this image has been magnified. This shows the problems which may be expected with an image whose pencils were initially so heavily layed out.

The fourth image was created by selecting all the white space, inverting this, and filling it with black. The pencils are creating a thickening of the lines and there are also some small marks and dots that may be the result of dirty paper or dust on the glass of the scanner. Selecting only the black lines on the third drawing and following the same method as previously described, we arrive at the final clean drawing. It should take less than a minute to adjust the levels, select the blacks, expand one pixel, feather 0.5 of a pixel, invert and fill with white.

This drawing was slightly more involved after the white fill, as minor corrections were needed on some of the more carefree inking.

So far we've used the computer purely as a tool for pre-print preparation. It can help us much more than this, but be warned: groovy-looking filters will never be a replacement for talent.

Bitmap

This is at the heart of the graphics processor. At the bitmap level, everything is reduced down to two simple instructions: on or off. These instructions tell the computer to make each pixel either black or white. There are no other choices.

Have a VERY close look at your local newspaper. Closely scrutinize the black and white images. Though they look like shades of gray, they are actually a collection of black and white dots. The realism and apparant variation is acheived by the accurate arrangement of these tiny dots.

Take a look at the image at right. This gives us a good sense of the importance of the frequency of the dots. The top wedge moves from four dots per centimeter through eight, 16, etc until the frequency is so high that it cannot be distinguished from gray. It also does this using all of the standard "halftone patterns" available in most graphics programs. From top to bottom they are: round, diamond, ellipse, line, square and cross. The standard one used to produce the graytone you see in Manga is round.

A crucial point to make here is the standard angle at which these dots are reproduced by the printing process. The standard in the West, though not in all countries, is 45 degrees. The reason this is so important is that if we print the dot pattern at a different angle to the one at which it was created, it will cause bizarre and unwanted patterns to form. These are known as moire patterns and can make

images look like an Op-Art experiment from hell.

Provided the above problems are kept in mind almost any tone we need for our Manga may be created, even the most subtle graduated ones. To the right the tone graduates from 100 to 0%. Old-school tone sheets were the only way to achieve this before the advent of personal computers. It's worth remembering that they work on exactly the same principle, reducing often graduating tones down to simple black or white dots. Many Manga artists still prefer to use these. One advantage is that they make for great-looking original art, the one-of-a-kind artwork you see displayed in galleries.

But doing it digitally gives us an unlimited palette, as well as unlimited control. We don't have to commit to anything until we're happy with the overall effect. We can also wait right up until the last area of tone goes down before converting it to bitmap.

Black and white printing is just that. Black ink. White paper. That's the grand total of the materials involved. Bitmapping is how we get the maximum result out of very little. Next time you're reading your favorite Manga and admire the artwork and depth of tone, lighting and shadows remind yourself that all you're looking at is a bunch of tiny, black dots on white paper.

Naked without tone

Now we may put this information to practical use. The images on these pages were done in grayscale mode. If your image is in color, you'd best convert it before continuing.

Use *Image/Mode/Grayscale*. Using a fairly standard character, we'll employ a wide variety of tones, using not just the bitmap function, but also something called *noise*.

For noise, think white noise, think pulling the arial out of the tv. This filter takes an image or selection and breaks it down from form into chaos. This can be a handy tool for generating particular textures and has a very different look and feel to regular bitmapping.

Step 1 shows the warrior character in nice, clean line form, ready for some tone to be applied. Needless to say, it's very important to make sure this image is as clean as practically possible before adding tone. We need the tone to fill right up to the black outline and not be broken up by areas of unerased pencil.

Step 2 shows the warrior with the first wave of tone applied. Here's how it's done:
First of all, make sure your background color is pure white.
Use the *magic wand* tool to select the areas you want to fill. Ensure the tolerance is high enough to reach the black outlines, but not so high it reaches outside. Using the color palette, select the tone you think is appropriate, then apply it using the airbrush.

Step 3 shows the same tone but

bitmapped. Using the magic wand, select all the graytone areas you've created. Select *copy*. Select *new*. This should bring up the new file window, with the size and dpi already in place. Select *OK*. This will give you a new window. Now select *paste*. You should get the graytone contents pasted into this new window. On your menu bar, select *Image/Mode/Bitmap*. This will bring up a options window. Make sure the resolution option shows the same value as the image you are working on. The bitmap method you need to select is *halftone screen*. Once you OK this, you'll get the halftone screen options, the first of which will probably be *frequency*.

You'll need to experiment with this in order to find the right size dot for your image. Try it at 40 dots per inch at first. If the result seems too fine or too course, adjust and try again. The next option is *angle*, which

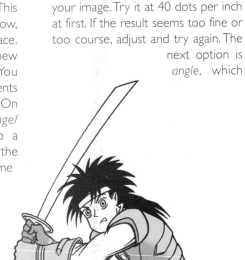

step 2

we have already discussed. Use 45 degrees. The last option is shape. Round is the norm, but try experimenting with the others if you wish. Click *OK*. We now have a bitmap version of our graytone. But we can't just paste this bitmap version straight onto out TIF file; first we have to convert it back to grayscale mode, so *Image/Mode/Grayscale*. You'll be asked for the size ratio. We don't want to change this, so use 1. Next we use a handy tool

step 1

Color basics in brief

At right is a *color wheel*. This device helps us work out the dynamics of color design.

At the circle's center are the three primary colors: blue, yellow and red. These are represented on the wheel but with the intermediate colors also displayed.

When one color faces another on the wheel they are known as *complementary* colors. This is because one color will be brought into stark relief by placing its opposite next to it.

Using the invert function in a graphics program immediately gives you a color's direct opposite. But keep in mind it will also give you its opposite luminance as well.

Using color creatively and effectively is largely a question of balance. Ultimately, if it *looks* good, it *is* good.

At right are a selection of *color on color* diagrams, showing the varying effects of surrounding one primary color with another. This can create optical illusions due to the power struggle involved. All the squares are exactly the same size.

Below is a diagram showing the CMYK colors, the basic building blocks of printer's color. They are represented first at 100 percent then decrease in strength by 20 percent increments.

You'll find something similar hidden in the folds of most cereal packaging etc. They are there as a guide for the printer. If the printed CMYK colors are right, then all's well; the package will be correctly printed.

Primary
Red,
blue,
yellow.

Secondary
Purple,
orange,
green.

Tertiary
Red-orange,
yellow-green,
blue-violet etc.

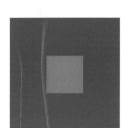
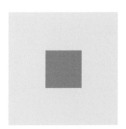
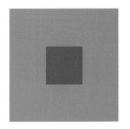
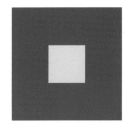

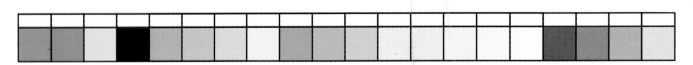

This page: a perfectly serviceable design for a Manga cover.
Opposite: the same components, but treated far more radically.

LIGHTING TREATMENTS
Above is an ambient lit figure. This approach is similar to that of natural sunlight.

Above is the same figure but lit simulating moonlight. The colors are desaturated and the contrast is reduced. The light source is completely ambient.

Above is a monochrome lit figure. Only the reds have been left unaffected. Although the hair looks white, it is in fact pink.

Here, a single light source illuminates the figure from the side. The long shadow indicates a low-lying light source.

EYE TREATMENTS

Every Manga artist has their own approach to rendering eyes in color.

Here, the iris first had graduated yellow/green tones applied. Note the tone is brightest at the center. The lowlights under the upper eyelid were then created.

A noise filter was then applied to the iris, followed by a mild gaussian blur. This gives a good, speckley effect similar to a real eye.

Lastly, the highlights were added with the simple use of an airbrush. The *hardness* level was set to 80.

1. Make sure the surface you want the water effect on is completely finished before you begin.

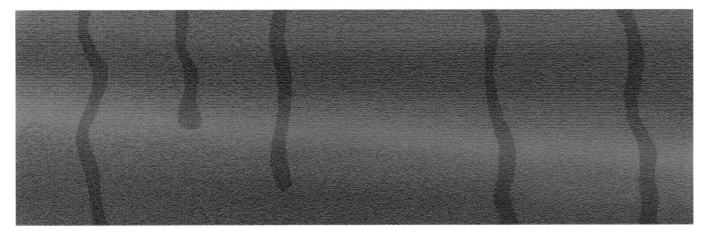

2. Water always deepens the tone of the surface on which it lies. Add this first, using the lasso and image adjust tools.

3. Next, add the highlights and shadows, paying attention to the direction of the light source.

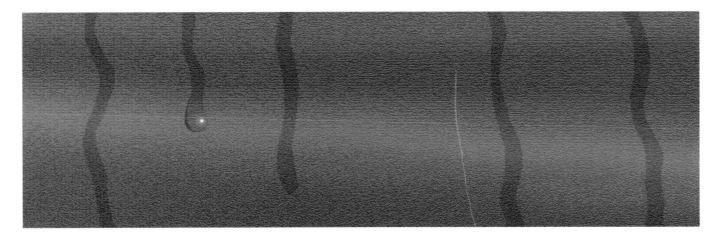

4. Finally, add a light reflection spot with the airbrush tool on pure white.

ADDING WATER EFFECTS TO COLOR

Effects in light

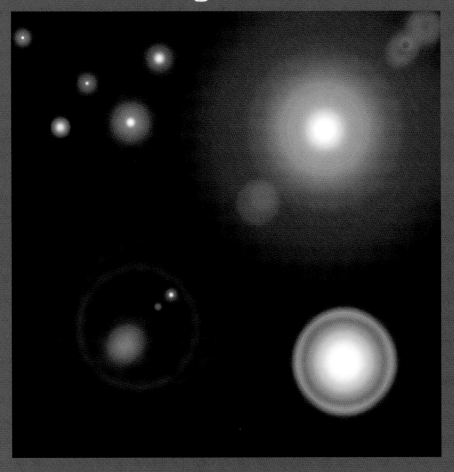

Lighting effects are pretty simple to master. In their most basic form they consist of two elements. Two shapes exactly the same in every way except for size. The smaller is slightly blurred and sits directly over the larger which is massively blurred. From this base we can start to experiment. There are a variety of ways we can blur things in most graphic programs. Then we could add a faint outline or overlay another blurred form.

The most common forms are lines or circles, but this need not restrict us.

Play around with form or color or the type of blur. The opacity level of a given layer is also important in the creation of the perfect effect.

Look at how other people have approached these effects. They should all be relativley easy to reproduce, once you understand these principles.

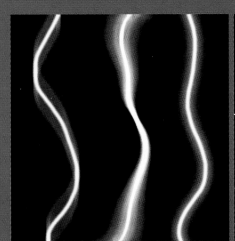

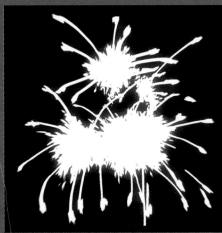

Photographs are a useful beginning when creating complicated abstracted backgrounds. These are great for high impact covers. But there are a few points to consider:

Whether mecha from crustations, dragons from lizards or in the case of the images on these pages, large interior spaces from real architecture, the use of real objects gives your mind points of reference that make your fantasy more believable. Manga often deals in abstracted forms of reality, so we need to abstract our backgrounds. Placing your characters directly over a photograph will make them sit on the surface of the image. Unifying the two requires bringing them stylistically closer together. When treating photos, a variety of blurs, transparencies and overlays help achieve this unity.

called *color range*. You'll find it in the *select* menu. You'll get a window with a sliding bar called "fuzziness." As we have only black or white on the canvas, this is more or less irrelevant. Zero is fine. Use the dropper tool to click anywhere where there is white. Click *OK*. Next, go back into the *Select* menu and choose *inverse*. This has the effect of selecting everything except the white areas. Select *copy*. Click back on your original file.

step 4

Step 4 shows the warriors tunic flat colored. We're going to use noise to alter this. Go to

step 3

The original graytone areas should still be selected. Delete these. This is why the background color was set to white. Now select *paste*. Our original flat grays have now been replaced with print-ready bitmap grays.

Filter/Noise/Add Noise to bring up the noise dialogue box. Crank up the amount slider to create some extreme white noise. Remember, we have to eliminate all grays. The higher the amount, the less chance of any grays

surviving. Have a close look at the noise you've created by zooming in. If you can see any gray pixels, select *ImageAdjust/Levels* and move the left hand input levels fader up until they turn black. If this produces too dark a color, try using the other faders to get a good balance.

Hopefully, you'll have something that resembles the effects in step 5. If all this seems to be really time consuming, remember that the more we use this process the faster it becomes. Doing large batches of grays at once will cut down on time.

step 5

In the chrome zone

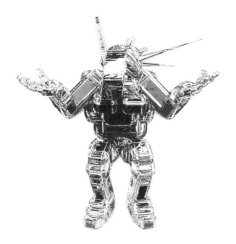

Making a metallic object actually look metallic can be tough when armed with nothing more than some black ink. Pretty decent-looking metallic effects may be achieved with just black alone, but when there is a graphics program to help out, we can really start to take things to the next level.

Before the machine is put to work we need to have a good look at what lies behind the illusion of metal.

Metal has two surface properties. The first is it's own color and tone, usually grayish. The second is reflection. This can vary from a dull, almost non-reflective surface right up to a near-perfect reflective quality similar to that of a mirror. Silver and gold when polished both have a very high reflection, but the pinnacle of mirroring is chrome.

Take a look at the image to the right. This barren, featureless landscape consists of sky, horizon and ground.

Imagine the dull landscape is reflected in a chrome ball. What would be different about the scene? As the

image below right shows, the shape of the ball would bend the light, curving the reflection to the shape of the sphere. This is the one essential thing to understand. What we see depends on a) what's reflected and b) what's doing the reflecting, in this case a chromium sphere.

At the top of the facing page is a basic human arm. There's no reason why we should not be able to turn this into a chrome arm using what we've learnt. We just have to remember: sky, horizon, ground.

Once the basic arm shape is drawn we have to decide where to put our horizon line and what kind of shape it's likely to have. When a complex shape like a human arm is chrome-plated, it can produce some pretty wild and unpredictable results. But the more our understanding grows, the more we can work in some of that unpredictability to our own drawings, helping them to look more convincing. With the horizon line established, we use a digital airbrush to mimic the sky and ground reflections, as the bottom image shows. It's very simple, but simulates chrome effectively.

Old style cars from the 50s through to the 70s are great for studying chrome reflections, as are many household objects. The curvier the better. Remember to simplifiy and boil down the information you get when observing chrome. It's surprising how little information is needed to convince the reader they are looking at a shiny metal object.

The sky, horizon and earth are things all of us see every day of our lives. We recognize them immediately on an unconscious level when we see them reflected in chrome. So it shouldn't surprise us too much that it's so easy to trigger that response by imitating only the most basic elements of what we see when we look at reflected metal.

It's for the same reason that the two colors used in almost every full color chrome reflection effect are blue above and brown below, with a black line separating them. The fact that this is not what we actually tend to see when we look at reflective metals is irrelevant. In almost all cases, even when doing interior scenes, this technique *works*.

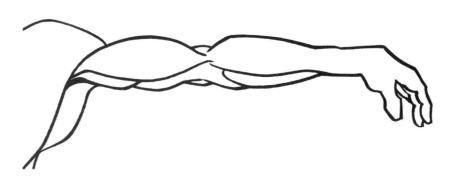

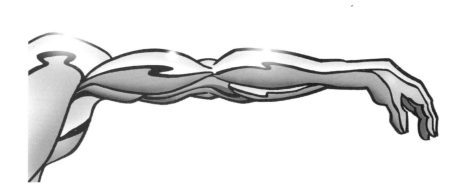

Analogue to digital

While graphics programs are undoubtedly extremely powerful, they are at their best when used in conjunction with actual drawing. Getting the best of both worlds can be an immensely satisfying experience, and this series of images aims to do just that. We're now going to use our knowledge of human anatomy to build on what we've just learned in the previous pages.

As before, it's the principles that are all-important. Learn these and we can chrome-effect anything we like.

But the process should only start once the basic figure is totally satisfactory.

Once the pose is right, mapping out of the light and dark areas commences. Does the light reflect, or is it unable to reach the area in question? These areas will by and large correspond to the main muscle areas and joints. These won't necessarily be the same as the final chrome effect lines, but they will act as a good guide as we plan the contours of the body.

The next stage gives anatomy knowledge a good workout. It's not enough to simply draw the body parts in with a few curvy lines. Imaginations need to be exercised to try and recreate the way that the light dances on this curvy, reflective surface. There are guidelines that are helpful: the larger, flatter areas of the body, such as the thighs and breasts will be relatively uninterrupted by lines, with large open areas. On the parts of the body where there are a lot of smaller muscles or ligaments,

the light will be thrown into more chaotic patterns. A case in point are the knees. Bone, ligament and muscle all join here, so expect a lot of detail. Using this technique helps bring out the actual shape of the body. Ideally, we should still be able to make sense

of the image even at the smallest thumbnail size.

When satisfied with the balance of the light and dark and our pencils are bringing out the curves and lines of the body, the ink comes out. The most important thing at this stage is to make sure we get smooth, flowing and flawless lines. As mentioned elsewhere, it's always a good idea to

give your hands a thorough clean before attempting to ink, especially with a job as delicate as this one. Thanks to technology, we can always correct any bumps or line wobble afterwards, but it's always better and less time consuming to get it right at this stage. Ink confidently and try some variety in the line width to give it life.

The picture on the facing page shows the character fully inked, without the black areas filled in. She already looks very "chromey." In fact we could just fill the blacks and leave it there, proving that you can indeed produce good-looking metal effects with nothing more than a black line. But let's go the whole hog and get the digital airbrush out.

First, a general body fill is done in a neutral gray tone. This will affect only the sections that are not enclosed by a specific shape. This neutral color

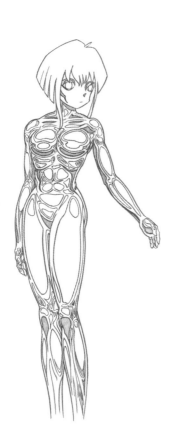

gives us something to work against as the darkest and lightest areas are mapped out.

Next we look at the largest shapes on the body, namely the thighs, breasts. arms and shins. These areas are used for a sky-like reflection, and the airbrush tool helps attain this. Note the shade of gray is a lot lighter than the general body gray tone.

The rest of the airbrushing is a question of judgement. As 90% of

the figure is filled, guage what's needed to create a balance to finish the job.

You may be wondering why the face hasn't been completely chromed. The complex form of the face would require a level of chroming similar to that of the knees. Although it may look impressive, it would also obscure a lot of character for ultimately no great benefit.

Making judgements about what to include and what to leave out is as big a part of the artist's job as anything else. Just because you *can* do something, it does not necessarily follow that you *should* do it.

This is an advantage that drawing will always have over photography and even over 3D programs. With a pencil in your hands, you decide exactly what should be included and excluded, right down to the tiniest detail.

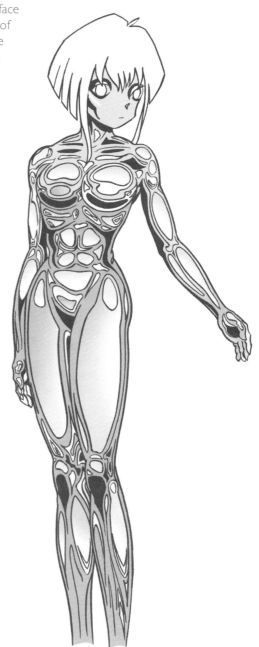

3

Light in composition

By putting everything we've learned in the last three chapters together an entire scene can be created. This will involve characters, backgrounds, lighting and toning.

It's hard to overstate the importance of good planning when constructing a reasonably complex scene such as this. Whatever we put down right at the outset will echo through the drawing, good or bad. So let's make sure we're happy with the basic breakdown. If we get this right, everything else should come easily.

We first have to decide on the content of the image. Then we have to do one of the most important things a Manga artist can do: *visualize*. Doodling and experimenting can often lead to good ideas. But the best way to proceed is to do absolutely nothing. Nothing, that is, until we have a clear vision in our heads of what the final image will look like.

Start by making a thumbnail sketch of the scene. An off-kilter angle adds drama. Then block in the main elements.

The scene involves a confrontation between a group of characters and an unknown enemy in a dimly lit

corridor. The lighting needs to be as dramatic as possible, but that has to have a source. With the side walls holding flourescent-type lightstrips, spooky single-source light can be introduced into the scene.

The drama can be heightened by almost blacking out the area behind the three main characters. This has the effect of trapping them between the unknown and the unfriendly.

All three figures are suspended in some kind of action, with the nearest, smallest figure gesturing to the others to hang back. This creates dynamic tension. A panel has come clean off the wall exposing the bare wires behind. Only one light seems to be functioning. All of this helps to create an atmosphere of an abandoned, dangerous place.

The only thing in the foreground is

the pair of hands with long fingernails. Not truly scary in themselves, but a sign that their owner stopped caring about their appearance some time ago.

Having given the "heroes" a wide variety of weapons, a laser sight is added to the nearest character's gun.

Because this image is to be fully toned in a graphics program, it's been inked without any areas of solid blacks. Doing this allows much more flexibility when making the final decisions about the lighting.

All of the inks are tight and will hold any tone when it comes to selecting the relevant areas.

The pencil undersketch was light, so once scanned the image was very quickly cleaned up.

Now for some tone. We should spend a little time doing nothing but look at the image, working out how to maximize its potential. What, if any, filters could be useful? What kind of shadows will the figures cast? What type of materials are the characters' clothes made of? This creates an approach to the whole image, not just one aspect of it.

The correct order to proceed once we've got a plan is:

Establish the basic tonal values of the

main characters. If they are pre-existing characters, a lot of this decision-making will have been done already, so start with the things we have no choice in. This will also include the near-black area behind the characters.

Firstly look at the tonal values for this scene. Once we have filled these in we'll have a better idea of how the image will work. With an image with such dramatic lighting it can be of great benefit to establish this before moving on to color.

One advantage of using a computer for toning is the ability to adjust or change anything. By working on separate layers in the graphics program we could easily create many variations and click through until the best one is found.

In progress

Having blocked out the most important tones it is time to look at what's left and decide on the most appropriate or complimentary flat colors, tones or patterns to balance the picture. Keep in mind that the more experimentation the larger our visual library of ideas will become and the more our art will reflect the journey we have taken and not that of another.

A slight mottling of the grays has been applied to the walls to give then a more interesting texture. Behind

the figures a cloud filter has been applied and adjusted. Eventually all the areas will be full and so comes the time to take a closer inspection. Zoom into the corners where one line meets another. This is often where white spots remain. These dots can be quickly painted with the appropriate color.

Only when we've got all of the above in place do we start to think about the lighting. Again, we should start with the things we have little or no choice in. The dark area where

the wires are coming from is a place to start.

The shadows in the last image over the page were made using the lasso tool, combined with the slight feathering of the line and a brightness/contrast adjust. This allows anything the shadow falls on to still be seen, albeit in much darker form.

Once the tones and shadows are put in place we should spend some time adjusting the image as a whole with levels or contrast. Sometimes

it's good to leave the image and return with fresh eyes. When we feel that everything's just perfect, move on to bitmapping.

Once again experiment with the style, mode and point size of the conversion until you arrive at the result you feel best suits the image. Obviously if you are producing a whole comic you will need to work consistently in order for the style to work as a whole.

Above is the finished image. If possible it is always a sensible idea to

make a good quality print of a finished image. This gives an opportunity to see the results clearly. Mistakes that may not show on screen are often glaringly obvious on paper. Also, it is useful to take on board the criticism of others. Accepting criticism is essential to gain greater perspective on your own work.

A crucial lesson to learn is to regularly save your work. Some programs can be instructed to do so every half an hour, but it's a good habit to train yourself to remember

to do this. If you are particularly pleased with the results make a hard copy. Back it up on a CD-R, floppy disc, or any format not contained on your hard drive. Losing a few hours work can be frustrating enough, if the graphics application decides to unexpectedly quit. But nothing can turn a peaceful computer artist into a homicidal maniac quicker than losing a week's work because the computer's hard drive corrupts.

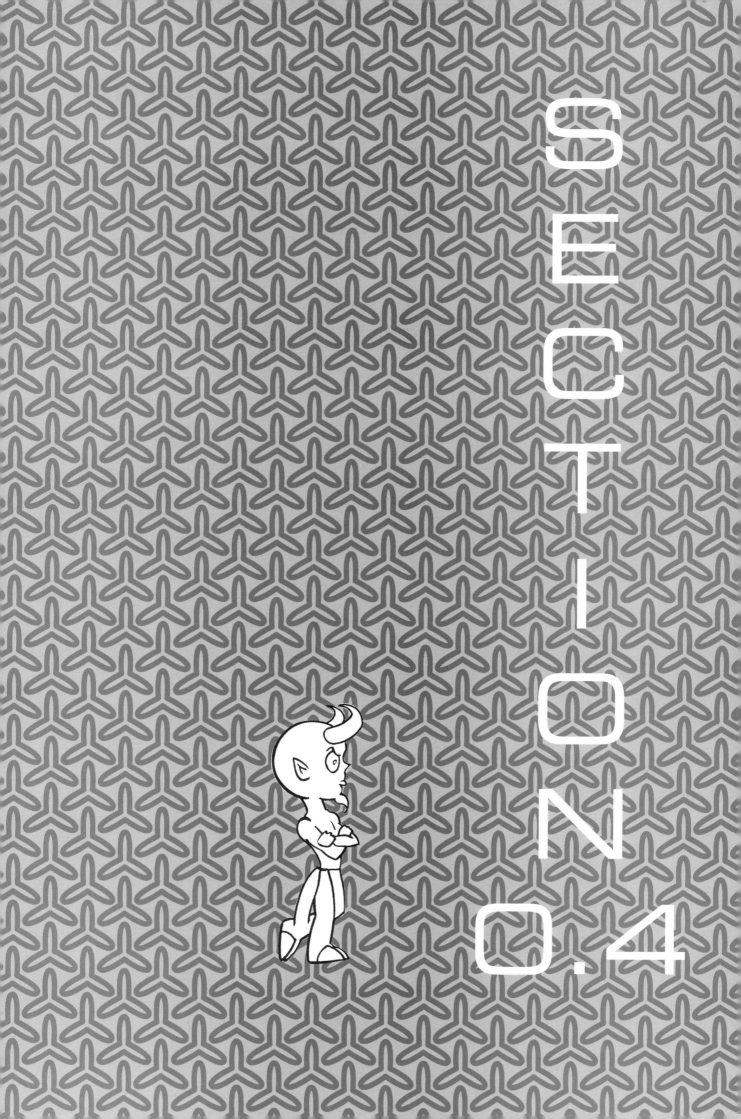

SECTION 0.4

Mech school

Since Astro Boy in the 60s, Manga and anime have explored the relationship between man and technology. Sometimes this investigation is purely for entertainment's sake, but just as often, Manga artists probe this man-machine topic with a seriousness worthy of the best science-fiction authors.

The possibilities of technology have been approached in Manga from many different angles. The most prominent sub-genre would have to be when technology goes out of control. This doesn't just mean rampaging 200 foot high mechas, though. Many of these storylines such as Masamune Shirow's *Ghost in the Shell* or Katsuhiro Otomo's *Akira* bring genuinely new insight into the subject, pointing out some of the potential misuses of technologies we are researching in the real world right now.

As a people living the most highly mechanized society on Earth, it's hardly surprising that it should be the Japanese who lead the world in fascination for the subject. Is the robot our friend because he does all the hard, manual labor for us? Or is he the enemy, making millions of workers redundant?

This chapter is all about the cast and crew of the technology-driven aspects of Manga; not only the Mechanoid and robotic type characters which populate them, but also how to develop vehicles and props of your own, using real-world sources as a starting point.

We're also going to take a look at building our own models, both physically and in 3D programs. These can be indispensable in working out problems, not only for basic drawing but also for lighting and dramatic angles.

Extrapolation

Imagination can be the greatest tool in creating our own mecha and hi-tech hardware. But to make them convincing, they have to look like they work. To achieve this, we have to find a real world starting point, something which already contains elements of what we want to depict.

Fortunately, there's a ready source for much of this information: the military.

The military's unquenchable thirst to find new uses for technology produces stunning examples of designs which have to be highly functional, as well as technologically advanced. Long-running concepts such as streamlining have been pushed to new extremes, resulting in highly futuristic designs.

By making an in-depth study of what already exists we are asking the all-important question: "What if?" What if we had the technology to produce fully mobile, bulletproof exo-skeletal suits? What if we built armored vehicles based on designs from nature? What if bio-tech enabled us to upgrade almost any of our body parts? All of these questions have been asked by Manga artists – and answered with some pretty wild results.

For inspirational material featuring some very different approaches to the subject, check out the following:

For bug and crustacean-based patrol vehicles see *Appleseed*, Shirow unashamedly bases many of his creations on crabs and spiders.

For mobile-suit type creations,

Patlabor is a great example. These human piloted mechas are brilliantly thought out.

For collosal mechanoid characters, *Neon Genesis Evangelion* features some extremely novel ideas about what controlling one of these massive, super-powerful mechas would entail.

The beautiful work of Takeshi Obata has an interesting take on the subject. Have a look at *Cyborg Grandpa G* for both great art and laughs!

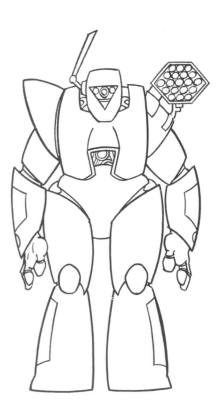

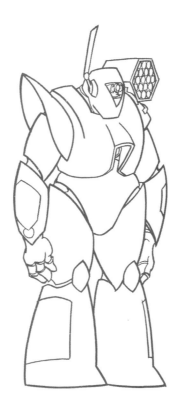

Flying in the real world

In the world of fast moving objects shape is everything. Most "plane spotting" books illustrate aircraft in silhouette. Imagine a very fast object at a great distance. It might have beautiful pattern work, decorating the body, but if you see more than a blurred outline then you are lucky.

So when you begin to draw any vehicle the most important thing is the shape. If you are a little unsure how to approach these types of drawing, remember the lessons we looked at in chapter two. Drawing from various angles can help us in our understanding of the object. Breaking it down into various simple forms and, placing those inside a cuboid means we can easily draw the shape from any angle. The only real way to master this is with lots of practice.

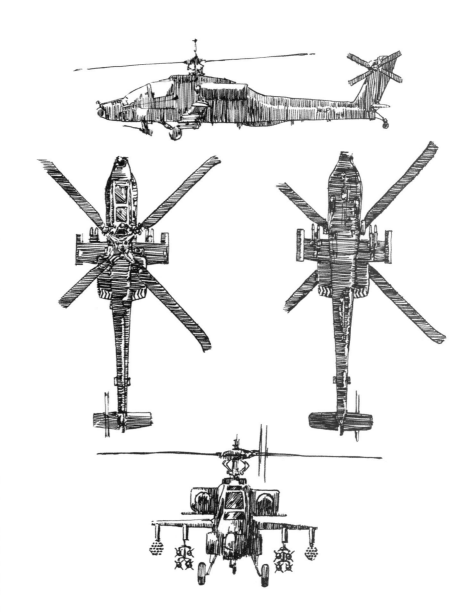

Once we feel comfortable with the shape we can start to work on detail. On a military vehicle the most distinctive details would be the weaponry. There are a lot of different types of this: Stinger missiles, sidewinder, cruise, patriot, scud missiles, machine guns, gattling guns, etc. Thankfully it all looks much the same and is relatively easy to draw. If you can draw ellipses and straight lines that's pretty much it. If you look at the apache helicopter to the right you should be able to make out the weaponry cradled under its wings.

One last important consideration is: How does it look when in motion? Helicopters have a characteristic tilt when flying. The nose dips and the tail rises and zoom.

The more you understand the physics of how a vehicle works the more believible you will be able to make it. The propellors practically suck the body upwards, so when racing forward it tilts and sucks itself along. Although now there are turbo rockets. The small propellors at the back of the craft stabalize it. If these are shot off or damaged then you can imagine the result.

One of the best ways to study these machines in action is at the movie theaters or on tv.

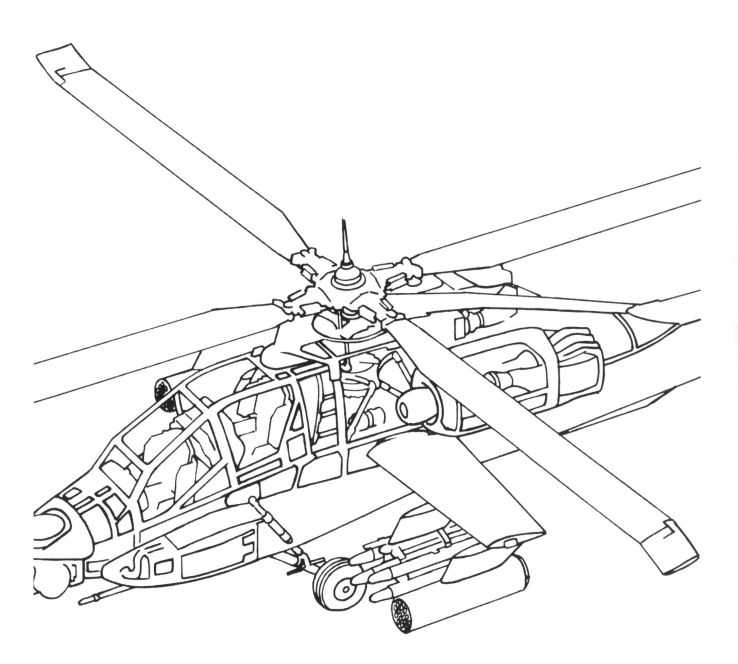

Getting more technically involved can be useful when machines feature heavily in your narrative. There are many books that give illustrated drawings and diagrams down to the smallest nut and bolt.

Choose your preferred vehicle and take a visit to your local library.

We should try to draw everything at once, working down in levels of detail. First the general shape, then a

more refined form, then the strongest details. Working too heavily on a single part might over balance an image, or worse, you may find the rest of the image is mysteriously out of proportion.

Things that go boom

Tanks are the ideal starting point when creating beefy, all-terrain vehicles. Some have the classic "tank tracks" wheel-and-belt style of motion, others have simpler eight or more wheel designs. They are, above all, practical designs with much to teach us about both stability and defense.

The more research into the features of these vehicles features we do, the better understanding we'll have of our own creations. Too often vehicles are drawn in a way that is superficially impressive, but on closer inspection incorporates non-functional junk. It's no coincidence that the most respected artists in Manga are the ones who've done their research.

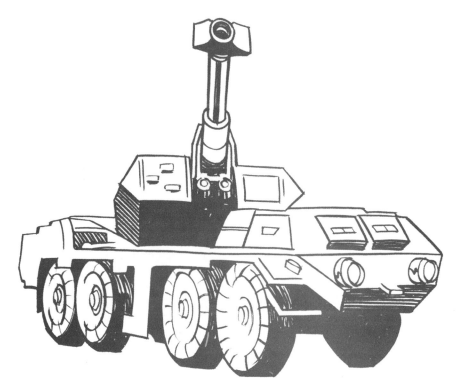

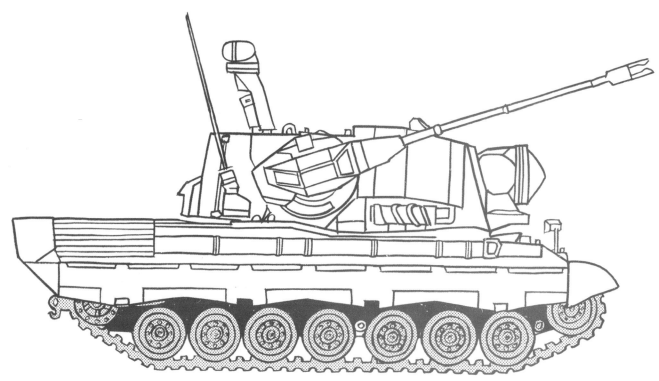

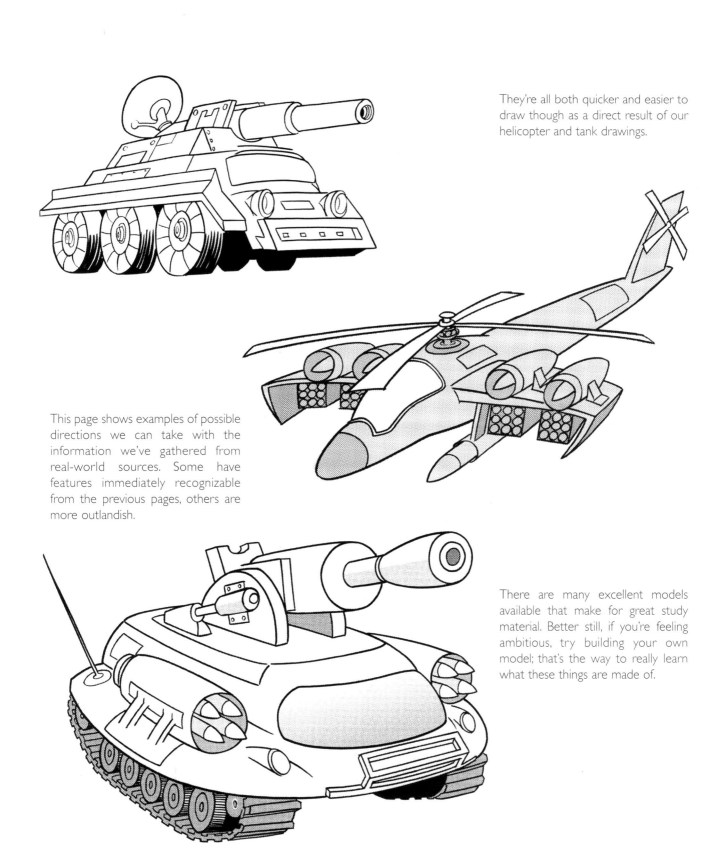

They're all both quicker and easier to draw though as a direct result of our helicopter and tank drawings.

This page shows examples of possible directions we can take with the information we've gathered from real-world sources. Some have features immediately recognizable from the previous pages, others are more outlandish.

There are many excellent models available that make for great study material. Better still, if you're feeling ambitious, try building your own model; that's the way to really learn what these things are made of.

Modeling

A subject too often overlooked in books of this nature is model building.

Not only do models provide a permanent source of reference for working out aspects of drawing, they also force us into a top-to-toe understanding of the mechanics and structure of the figure or vehicle. With this kind of information at our fingertips, we are adding another powerful weapon to the arsenal of drawing tools.

You needn't build something as complex as the images on these pages. A simpler maquette, or basic posable figure without all the detail can be just as useful.

The model you see here was constructed by a professional with many years' experience. This doesn't mean it was expensive or made from highly specialized parts. On the contrary, many of the features started life as objects as mundane as the lid of a super-glue tube. It's amazing what can be creatively transformed if our imaginations are really engaged.

The sketches at right are just that; rough ideas given to the model-maker as a starting point. These drawings don't need to be technical masterpieces, especially as we wished to allow the model-maker room to bring his own ideas to the model's designs.

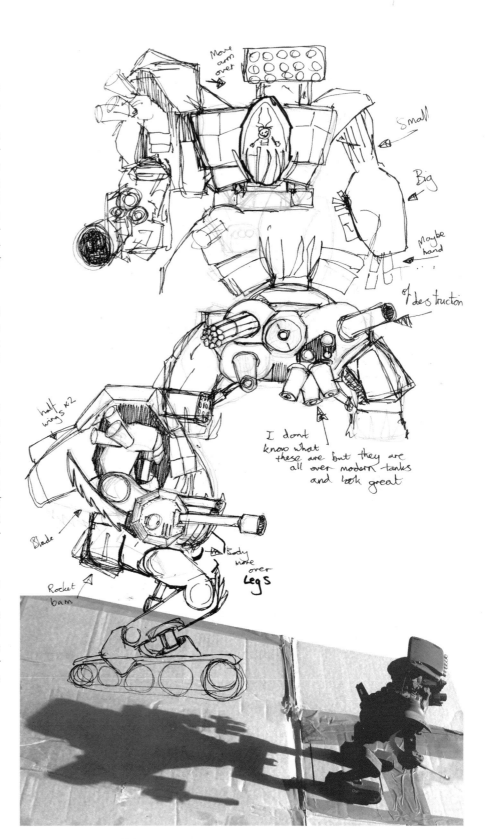

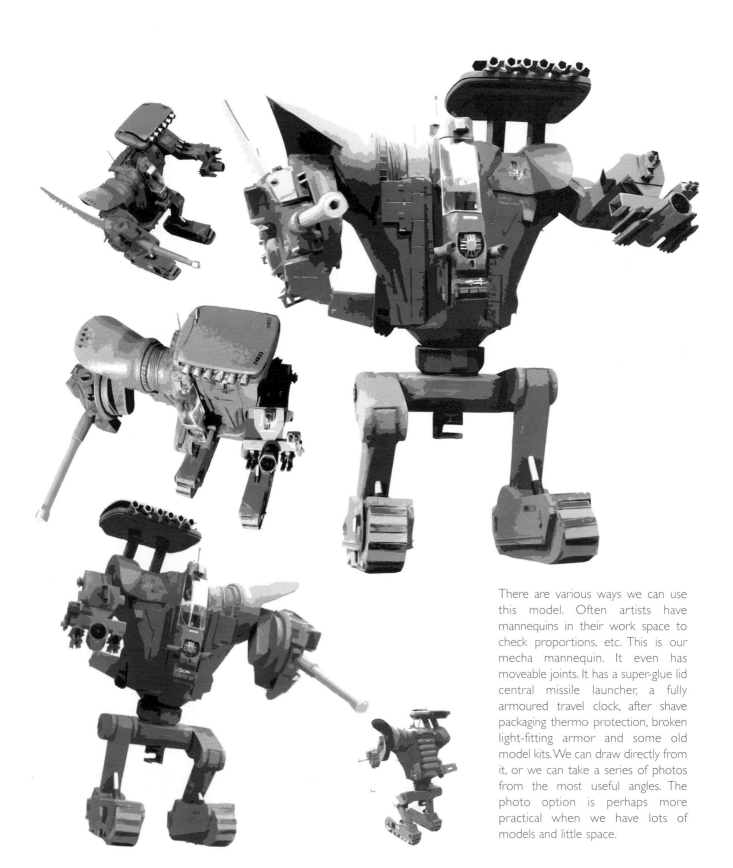

There are various ways we can use this model. Often artists have mannequins in their work space to check proportions, etc. This is our mecha mannequin. It even has moveable joints. It has a super-glue lid central missile launcher, a fully armoured travel clock, after shave packaging thermo protection, broken light-fitting armor and some old model kits. We can draw directly from it, or we can take a series of photos from the most useful angles. The photo option is perhaps more practical when we have lots of models and little space.

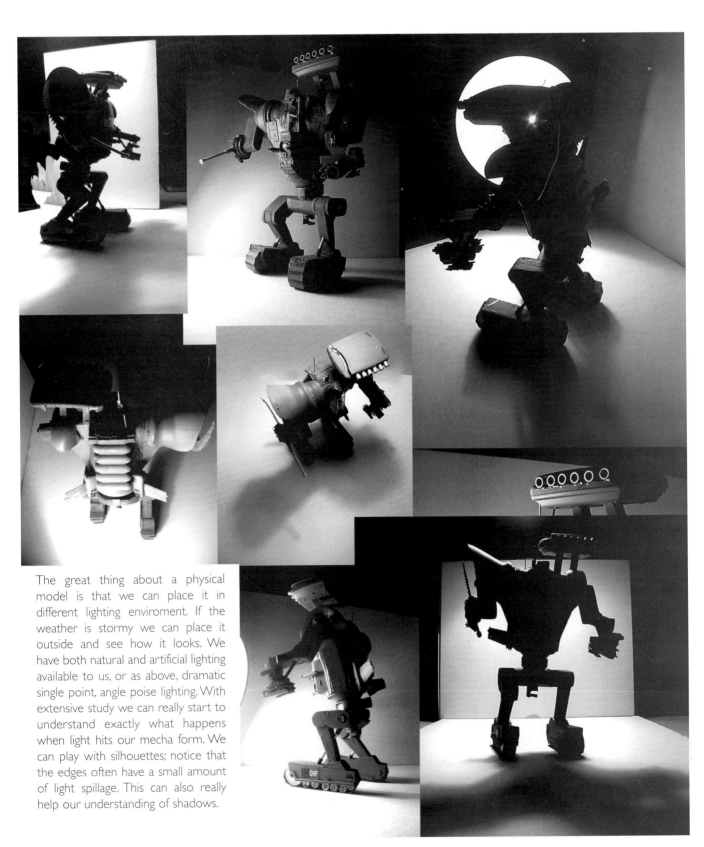

The great thing about a physical model is that we can place it in different lighting enviroment. If the weather is stormy we can place it outside and see how it looks. We have both natural and artificial lighting available to us, or as above, dramatic single point, angle poise lighting. With extensive study we can really start to understand exactly what happens when light hits our mecha form. We can play with silhouettes; notice that the edges often have a small amount of light spillage. This can also really help our understanding of shadows.

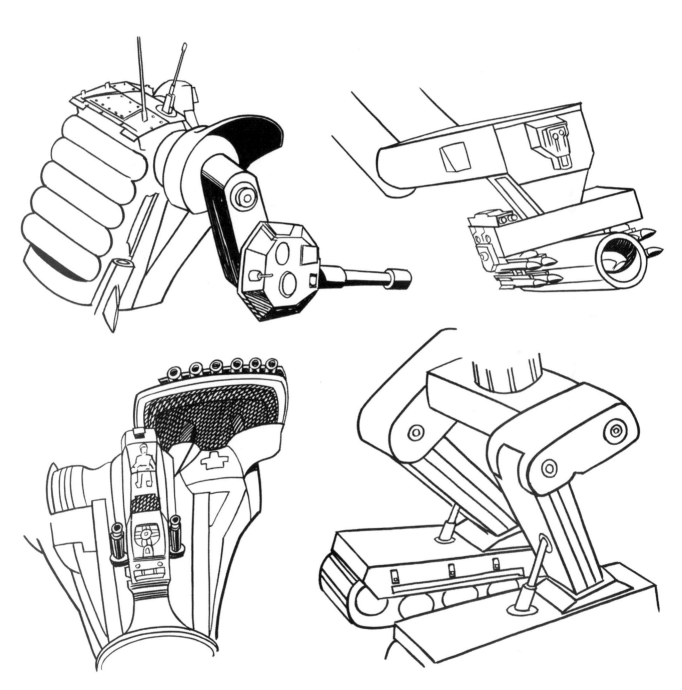

From all this we can begin an inventive study of our mech warrior, looking at specific areas. Creating features on the plastic shell, smoothing off the rough areas, adding pertinent details. These studies should slowly bring our model to life. Eventually we will no longer need the model, as all the information concerning form will hopefully be transferred to memory. We'll understand how light hits the form and shadows are cast. The greatest benefit of this work, however, comes from the happy accident. Suddenly, we discover an interesting angle or cool bit of lighting that without this journey wouldn't have been possible.

Creepy-crawly

Designers have always looked to nature for new approaches to dynamics. After all, nature has had millions of years to work out the ultimate streamlining for particular designs and tends to make some of man's efforts look pretty crude by comparison.

Nature's designs are based primarily on function. This means the best design for the job they have to do. Anything superflous has been stripped away.

A shark's body is incredibly streamlined. It's primary function is a simple one; to obtain food as quickly and efficiently as possible. A hawk's body is a more complicated design, with good reason. One of its functions is to hover as it searches for prey. This means it has to stay aloft with the minimum of effort. Once the quarry is sighted however, the hawk can change body shape by closing its wings and plummeting at high velocity towards its prey.

The complexity of a creature or mechanoid is dependent on functions. As we design a new creation we should be asking ourselves: "What is this creation's purpose? What functions will it have to perform?".

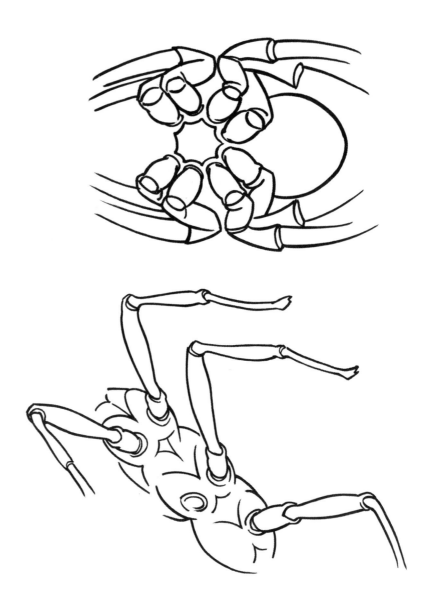

The major feature of most mechanoids in Manga is the exo-skeleton, a form of armored skin. Most of the information about how such a tough outer layer might fit together has been taken from the real world, in particular crustacea and arachnids, as well as other insects. The drawings on this page are studies of the particularly pertinent parts. Once again, nature is way ahead of us in the design. The most stunningly inventive parts are the articulation of the limbs. As a tough outer shell will naturally limit the amount of movement available, nature has contrived a system of articulation based on a combination system. Look at the way the spider's legs above top are organized. All the joints have quite a small amount of movement available to them. But this is offset by the fact that it has many joints articulated in different directions. Through a combination of differently oriented joints, a surprisingly large amount of movement is possible.

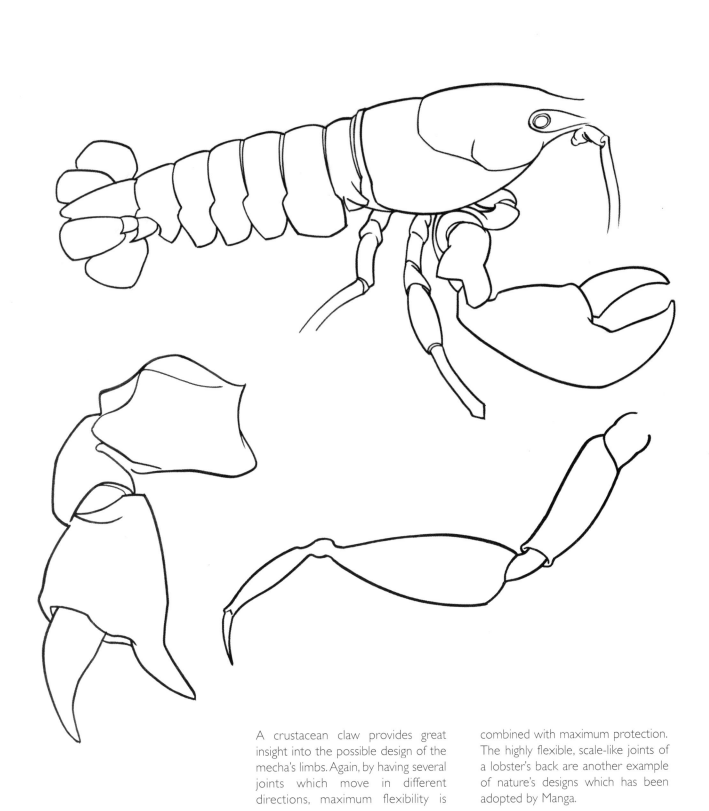

A crustacean claw provides great insight into the possible design of the mecha's limbs. Again, by having several joints which move in different directions, maximum flexibility is combined with maximum protection. The highly flexible, scale-like joints of a lobster's back are another example of nature's designs which has been adopted by Manga.

From spider to battle vehicle

The drawings on these pages are all extrapolations, which is to say they have all been inspired by nature's designs. These have been co-opted for entirely different uses, but their source is still evident, especially in the image immediately at right.

Some of the others are not quite so glaringly obvious but nonetheless display an understanding of the natural design principles involved.

To create a four-armed, exo-skeletal police unit, it is necessary to know something about how nature would do it.

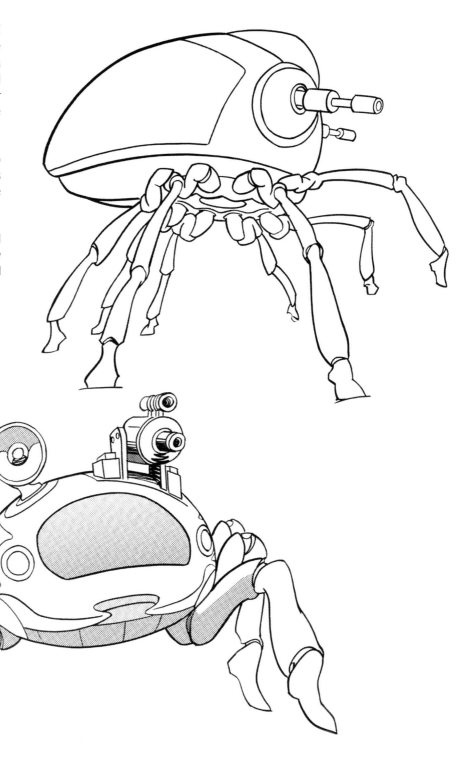

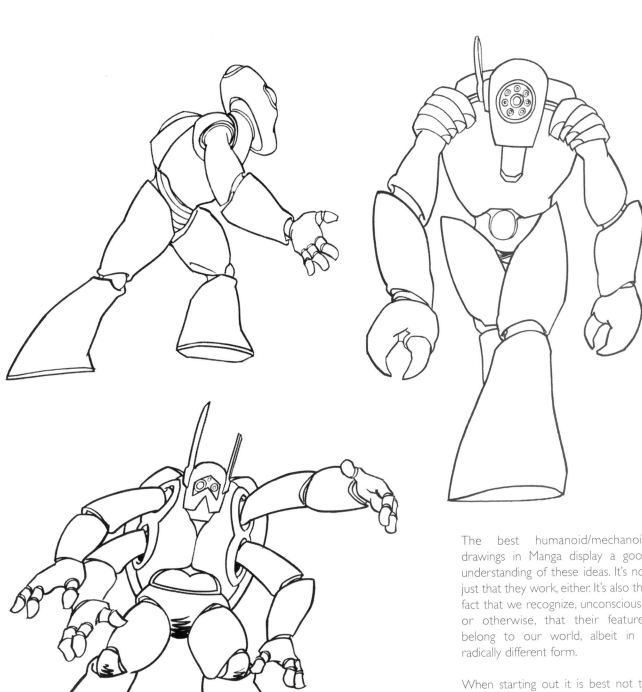

The best humanoid/mechanoid drawings in Manga display a good understanding of these ideas. It's not just that they work, either. It's also the fact that we recognize, unconsciously or otherwise, that their features belong to our world, albeit in a radically different form.

When starting out it is best not to spend too much time on individual drawings. Try alternating between drawing crustacea and drawing mechanoid types. This will keep the information fresh in your mind until you have it stored permanantly.

Other peoples scribbles

We can often get stuck in our own rut, repeating the same ideas. Not only is this potentially boring, it's a sure sign that we may be temporarily stagnating.

This is where fellow artists come into their own. Every artist has their own motifs and specialities. They will always be able to give a different take on things.

If you're lucky, you'll have a friend or associate you can exchange ideas with. Failing that, start looking outside your usual stable of favorite artists for inspiration. When you see something you like, pull it apart and try to figure out why it has that effect on you. We have a natural tendency to particularly admire work whose techniques are not well understood to us.

This page shows an associate's take on mecha; quite different in style and construction to the rest of the book. When we do this exercise we can't help filtering the approach through our own experience and techniques. After all, we are not aiming to copy but take part in a hopefully rich exchange of ideas.

On the opposite page, the favored elements of the original artist's drawings have been brought out. Likewise, the elements that may have been less appropriate have been diminished or cut out altogether.

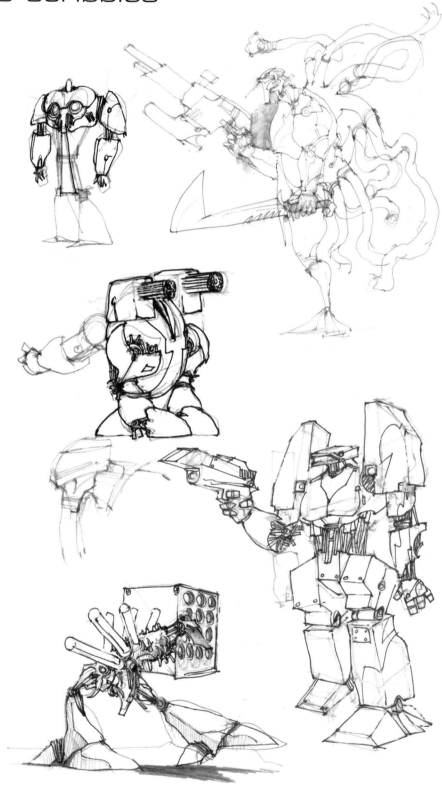

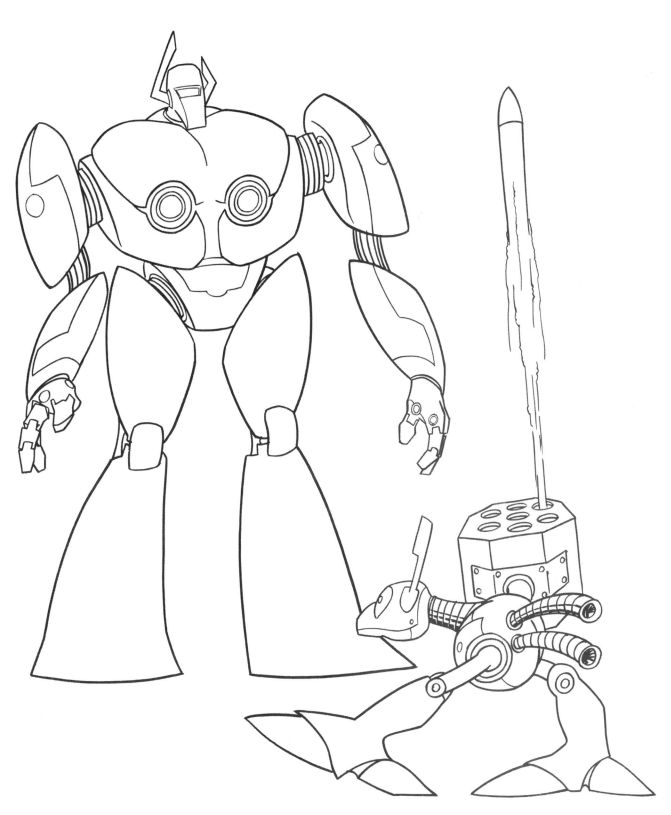

3D inspiration

For those with a desire to spend hours at a computer screen instead of hunched over a drawing pad, 3D graphics are another great way to both try out new ideas and build models from which to work.

The images on this page have been rendered using a light-particle imitating process known as raytracing. This gives an accurate idea of such features as light and reflection. Not only can we change the position of the model, we can also add or remove lighting, and change the model's "skin" or superficial appearance.

The figure at right has been rendered in several different ways throughout this book. This demonstrates the flexibility of the 3D approach.

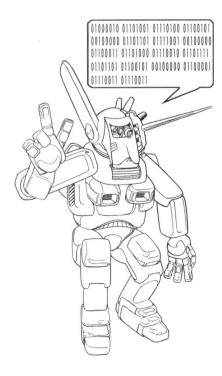

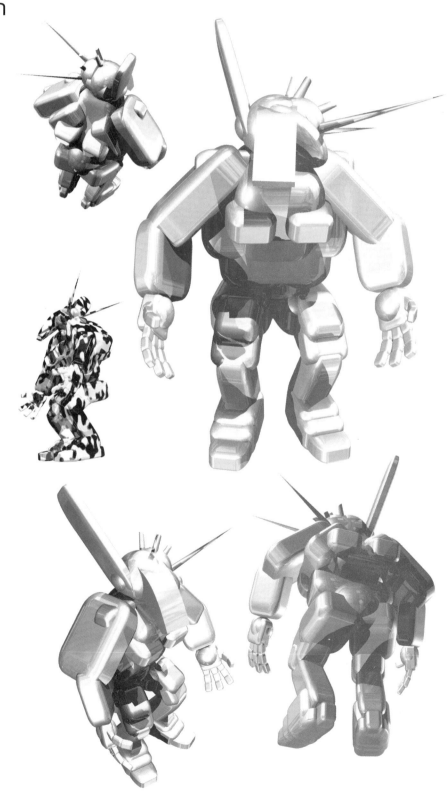

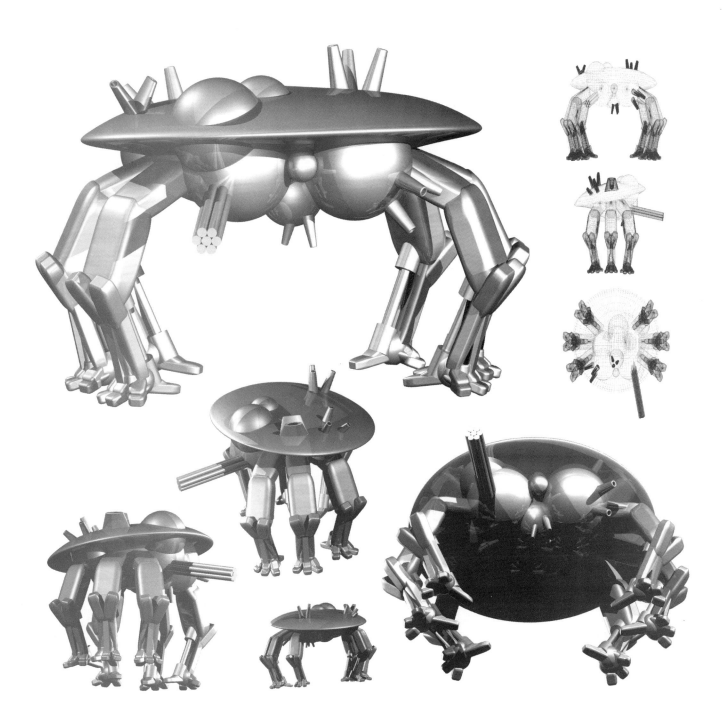

With something as complex as a six-legged mecha-monster, a 3D model really comes into its own.

It should always be borne in mind that these types of model are useful only as a starting point. It's a bad idea to become reliant on these as an end product. Always keep in mind that you are telling a story. The best way to do this is to bring as much humanity and expression to bear as possible.

Keep detail to a minimum, as this not only takes up too much time and memory, but you, the artist is simply much better at that job.

125

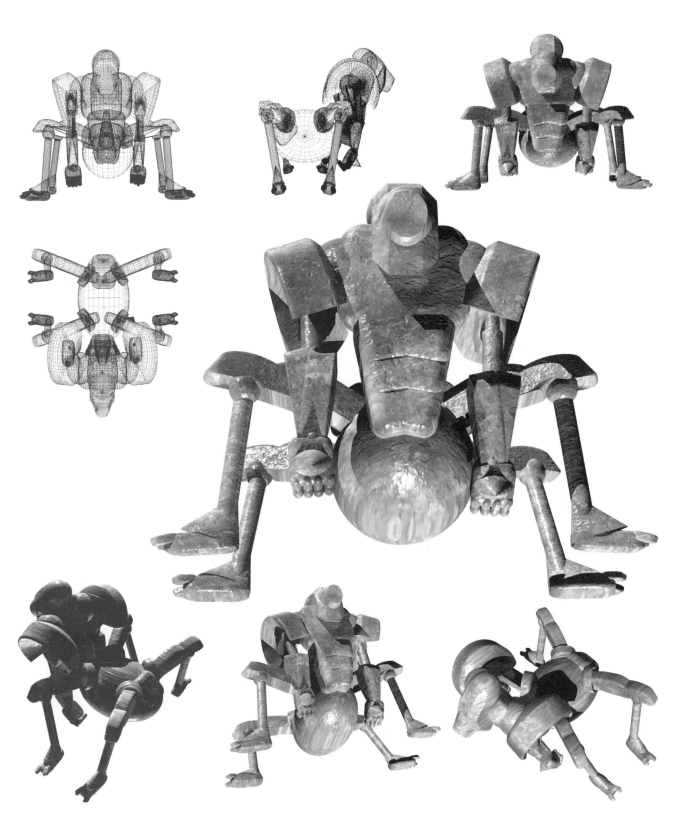

4

Mecha out of the machine

These next two pages include examples of what has been discussed in this chapter. We start with a rough idea of what we want to create in a 3D program.

Next comes the actual construction of the 3D design. Fortunately there are a plethora of publications on the subject, as well as manuals that come with the leading software.

When we're happy with the construction of the mecha, we'll light him appropriately and deliver the angle we need to draw him correctly.

The reference can now be used direct from the screen, or if we prefer, a printout can be made to work from. These is often more useful, due to ease of manipulation.

On the page opposite is the result of this modeling and attention to detail, a full-blown page of Manga featuring our newly created mechanoid.

Nature, super-glue tubes and 3D programs. Just some of the tools and approaches at our disposal to raise inspiration levels up to their potential.

Remember, there's nothing like a small dose of reality to make fictional creations that much more alive.

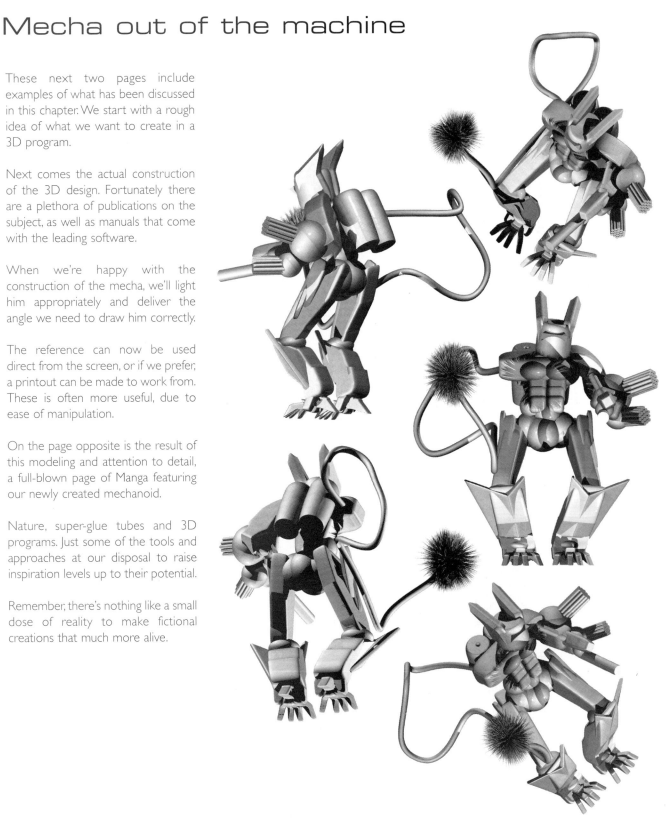

SECTION 0.5

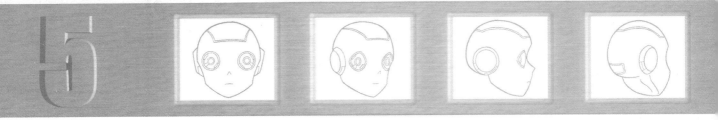

Graphic innovation

Perhaps the most striking distinction between Western comics and Manga is in attitude to design. Western comics have from time to time enjoyed occasional upheavals in graphic approach, the late 60s and early 70s come to mind, but Manga's design revolution appears to be constant. New concepts in image presentation appear annually constantly challenging previous ideas as to what is acceptable or possible.

With Manga, you really can do anything you like with the design. The only criteria are that it should be visually arresting and work.

No element of the design is left unexplored, from the panel layout to panel shape. Sometimes there are no panels at all. Within the Manga world there is a huge range of diversity. Drawings at one extreme that are pure outline and at the other extreme solid blacks and whites. Between these, there is every shade of gray. The approaches vary from the traditional chinese charcoal ink of Reiko Okano to the Aubrey Beardsley-style explored by Mineo Maya. There is the stark and stylized world of Blame by Tsutomu Nihei or the childlike drawings, complete with color crayons, of Saho Tono.

The larger Western comics companies have traditionally had a "house style" where the company's graphic look is formularized. An editor oversees the artist's style in order to create consistency within the "brand." While this easily identifies a company's product to the consumer at the newsstand or comic store, it has a tendency to stifle graphic innovation and is ultimately at odds with the notion of constant change.

Looking through a stack of random Manga, there is little or no evidence of this approach. Wild and daring ideas assault our senses as we go from one title to the next.

But design has to work. This chapter looks at what underpins Manga's radical approach.

Panelology

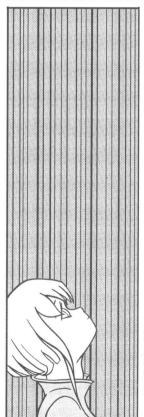

As the most basic unit of Manga, the panel's content is limited only by the restraints and needs of the story and our creativity.

A single page may contain anything from one to 100 panels. They might be part of a fluid storyline, or in extreme cases made to be viewed simultaneously.

Even in non-linear storylines the panels have to connect to each other, building concepts for the reader as they progress.

Size is also an important consideration. As a rough guide, larger spaces favor key images and pivotal moments in the story. Size also affects the pacing of a story. Unlike film, where the image size is constant, Manga has the added devices of size and shape. When used creatively, this creates extremely powerful effects like no other medium.

Often the panel acts as little more than a placemat for the image. The artwork spills out from every angle and the border is barely visible behind all the action. Alternatively, a thick black boarder will oppressively hem the image.

In Manga we find all aspects of layout and design pushed to the limit. Every extreme is explored and stretched. In graphic experimentation alone Manga wipes the floor with other comic forms and even much commercial graphic design.

On a most basic level

The page layout is an integral part of the story. It influences how we read the page and to some extent how we approach the content. It is a subtle method of style because it is often not consciously noted.

Like everything in Manga, almost anything goes. From a quiet, even repetition to a fractured chaos, the drawings at the right skim through a range of approaches. The only question we need to ask ourselves when drawing a strip is; what layout best suits what I am trying to communicate? We should trust our own instincts and go with what we feel.

Line A breaks the layout into even regular boxes, arranged in lines of four. Although there are other factors specifically, the amount of text and detail – the size of the box sets the pace. Small boxes are more stacatto and longer panels more sustained. A rectangle that stretches over several lines will naturally command more attention than anything smaller.

As we see in Line B, if we alter the borders horizontally and/or vertically the pages become more dynamic. This is clearly seen in the last in the sequence; the panels seem to tumble down the page.

Line C is more weightless and free floating in composition.

The final line (D) of pages takes a more extreme approach, which poses quite a challenge for the reader but can be rewarding.

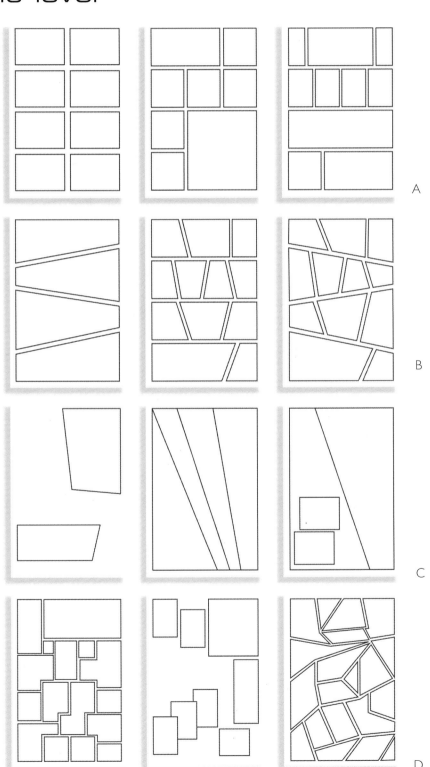

Breaking the boundaries

At right are four common examples of how layout is pushed to extremes when a central character is tucked behind, stands in front of, leaps out of, or even uses the panels as cover.

This composition adds huge depth to a page. Traditionally the panel contains the image, acting as a regulator of pace. With this more free-form approach, the boundaries have been removed. The composition of the page is as important as that of an individual panel. Because of this, Manga is often more visually arresting than its Western counterparts.

In image A, the figure stands in the background. Although she occupies the majority of the page, she is less important than the overlapping panels.

With image B we have just the opposite, giving her prominence over the panels. Thinking of a stage with characters and scenery is often useful when approaching such arrangments.

On page C the character is leaping from the panel, directly at the reader. This give the sense of actually being involved in the action, and helps draw the ready into the story.

Page D plays with concepts. It is a visual joke so that the gun-blasting character is using the foreground panels as cover. The panel in which she stands could be removed altogether, but the tension created by the restriction adds to the scene.

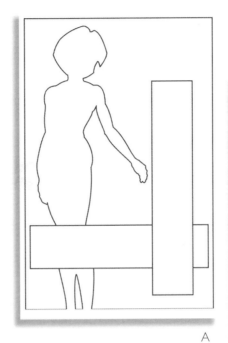

A

B

C

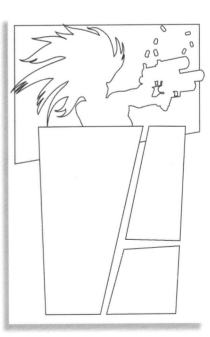

D

5

Patterns

Another common feature is the use of full-bleed patterned backgrounds. These are very often abstracted as in picture B. Or they partially abstract like A and C, or symbolic as in D.

Clouds, smoke or mist are emotive, and commonplace in certain styles of Manga. The first image has brooding clouds atop a graduated tone. This sets a dramatic scene upon which our sword swinging lady is in full action.

The second image uses the technique of marbling to create an abstract and swirling backdrop to the panels. Depending on the style or intensity such abstractions can create interesting atmospheres. This is an example of craft and design that is not usually associated with comics. Such integration is prominent in a lot of Manga. For those wishing to expand their visual repetoire there is a brief description of how to make marbled paper in the glossary.

Gradients such as those in the third page are often decorated with symbolic items pertinent to the narrative. Flowers are particularly common, as one would expect, in the more romantically themed titles.

The final image creates drama. The central circular panel is symbolic of the moon. The pure black surrounding only serves to emphasize the silhouetted figure.

Anything that can be used to add atmosphere or subtly reinforce the narrative may be used.

A

B

C

D

Speed lines

Manga is synonymous with speed lines. They are probably the most prominent and commonly used device in the field, and are essential in conveying action.

One problem can be creating a sense of motion in a static image. A directional blurring looks great but is relatively expensive to reproduce effectively. Comics are not generally reproduced at 600 dpi on high quality paper. This is where speed lines come in. In Manga, these have evolved into an artform within an artform.

In the strip at right the speed lines create a windy forest scene. They show the curling motion of a single leaf in the storm, and below that a man struggling through the miserable weather. As he runs, the blackness from which he comes creates both a sense of foreboding as well as a feeling of motion. The next panel is small, and superflous detail has been stripped from the image. Only his head and the speed lines that emanate from a central point are present. This shows a split-second of shock. The speed lines then go on to describe the motion of a sword blade as the hero ducks just in time. The speed line separates him from a small piece of his hair. In the last panel, we see the motion of the hero as he leaps into action, as well as the point of impact of where foot meets chin.

When working with speed lines, work quickly. To convey the feeling of speed, use speed.

Composition in tone

When starting out, we are often under the impression that some artists use an incredible amout of scatchy detail. This is sometimes the case, but we need to be aware that the artwork has usually been greatly reduced.

It is normal to assume that most artwork is reduced when printed. This reduction tightens the work making it more compact and dynamic. If it has too much minute detail then this will be lost, or worse still, corrupted. This needs to be worked into the equation when planning composition.

With the most simple line drawing, our only worry is that the line thickness is not too delicate. With bold images where only light and dark are depicted in pure black or pure white, our only concern is that there is no area of either shade that's too small. With pages of various shades of gray however, we need to be a little more careful.

Images with little contrast can be difficult for the reader to decipher, and printing can exacerbate this. Put simply, an image that has strong impact is one which is clear. Although the background of the flying bunny to the right is very detailed, the character is still conspicuous against it. Contrast in this sense should not just applied in terms of tone. Anything which increases the difference between that which is important for a scene and that which is superfluous is good. In some Manga after the first establishing scene, background is removed altogether.

Speech

As with everything else in Manga, speech balloons have taken on a life of their own. Like most Western comics, Manga artists employ bubbles containing dialogue. However the approach is often far more adventurous.

Western dialogue balloons, or speech bubbles, tend to be extremely formulaic. In the West there is little innovation from one publisher to the next, let alone between titles.

The dialogue boxes at right help press home the type of character connected to them. The shapes also help convey the emotional content of the words. They should balance well with the backdrop on which they will inevitably sit and also should enhance the message.

So let's break our approach into two basic considerations:

What shape or frame will best communicate the emotion and/or text for this character?

What will be most suitable for the context of the scene?

obviously the text goes into the center of the boxes and bubbles...

139

Typography

Many exhaustive volumes have been written on typography. But what is its relevance to the art of Manga?

Until the arrival of Americans after WWII, graphic design as we know it did not exist in Japan. But the US forces introduced many new consumer goods, including packaged products and their brand of comics. These foreign ideas were adopted and then adapted to suit Japanese tastes. Naturally enough, the Japanese take on the concept of design was a radical· departure from the American approach. Since that time there has been an incredible creative explosion in design.

As we already know, Manga has few boundaries. The rule is; if it works, do it!

So what is the best way to approach this vast subject? Most text in comics is hand written, but for the sake of analysis let's look at a stencil font. We'll break down the approach into principles that can be applied as a general rule.

A lot of the "feel" of a font comes from association. The font below is synonymous with the military. This came about for purely practical reasons, adopted as it was by the army to label property and is easily applied through a stencil with spray paint. It is a legible script, and, because this style has been in use for over 70 years, its form carries a message by association.

Of course, stencil type is more widely used than just the military. In logistics, companies also label containers with this. The message is "Items for transportation or storage that belong to a large organization".

Different typefaces have associations with different things. The world of graphic design is about using this to inform and entice people by communicating via the form of the letters as much as the meaning of the words.

The fun starts when we have enough knowledge to start to play with these associations. The British Graffiti artist, Banksy, is well know for his subversive

stencil art which has appeared in streets all over the world. Clever parody can subvert the original message of a type face to add levels of humor or irony to your work.

Sadly, in most Manga translations the original text is replaced with a bland Western style which distances us from the artist's original vision.

Try to become aware of the responses triggered by particular styles. And remember, above all, the text must be legible.

STENCIL FONT

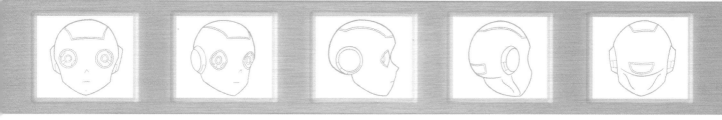

Blow them off the page

Typography used for sound effects is generally done by hand. It is almost inconceivable that computers will ever exert the control and flexibility necessary to tailor particular sounds to the need of a particular panel.

A computer can be useful in pasting the sound effect onto the page. If we use this method, rather than penciling along with the rest of the graphics, there is more choice over positioning and scale.

The pencils here start out quite plain, with the shape and positioning of the letters worked out. As this first sound effect is for an explosion, the letters have to look as though they are reacting to the explosion, almost like they're being blown off the page.

The next stage is treatment. Depending on the context there are several treatments used for explosions. This is a "quake" type, where the outline of the letters is echoed with further lines.

The second sound effect is quite different. It could be used for boots on gravel, or even a dragon crunching bones. Again, the look should fit the sound. Compressing the letters aids the effect, as does the jagged finish of the outline and the up-down positioning of the individual letters.

Boom

In Manga there are certain iconographic elements. These appear with more or less frequency depending on the chosen genre. Smoke and explosions are two of the most notable.

Although each artist has their own approach, smoke and explosions follow the same basic patterns.

Obtaining the shape of billowing cloud is not difficult. Photographic references can be helpful. The key thing is to keep in mind is that a *mass* is being drawn. The line should describe the form. Shadow is optional and the strength depends on lighting.

An explosion is a rapid release of energy, usually involving a bright single light source. In the rapid expansion, dust and debris will be whipped up into billows. With a strong light the contrast will also increase. The areas of the cloud which cannot be reached by light will be dark while those touched by the blinding light will be light.

Artists who excel at smoke and explosions include Katsuhiro Otomo, most famous for *Akira*; Tsutomu Nihei, *Blame!*; and Masamune Shirow, *Appleseed*, *Dominion* and *Ghost in the shell*.

The real deal

We've covered the general points of page layout, and discussed some of the more common approaches to patterned backgrounds. We've looked at some of the uses of speed lines, and considered various approaches to typography and how best to use it. Then there are the frames that surround our text, if any, and how they effect our reading of it. We have also covered basic principles of panel composition, line strength and image balance.

There is no formula or defining method for layout. One of the most exciting aspects of Manga is its constant evolution. In Western comics innovation and experimentation are generally only found in the underground comic scene. In Manga it's everywhere! It would be wrong to attempt to squash the Manga approach into a formula. Such definitions close off new possibilities, when we should be trying to open them.

If you haven't come across much genuine Japanese Manga before, seek it out. You don't have to speak Japanese to appreciate the impact of this unadulterated version of the design. There are several good books printing the 'real deal', as well as several magazines which go to great lengths to mess with the original as little as possible. See the back pages of this book for more details.

Over the next two pages we'll break down the construction of a simple Manga page and see what can be learned.

From thumbnail to finish

Now let's try to use everything we've learned so far to assemble a full-blown page of Manga. The example here is from page 19 of "Monkeypop Terminal". This is a pivotal page which uses key design elements, sound effects and dialogue.

The image below is what is known as a "thumbnail" sketch. Its purpose is to work out the general layout and dynamics of a page. Most of the information and design works, but

notice a few small changes to the final finished pencils, at right.

The blast from the cannon works better when coming from the same direction as the previous panel. Another sound effect has been added. The other changes are more minor and concern much smaller adjustments.

Opposite is the final version: inked, lettered, toned and ready for print.

The use of diagonals in the panels is not simply a design conceit. For instance, by giving more space to the left-hand side of the top panel, there is more room to the character "Gogs" and less for unimportant detail.

As the page climaxes with an explosion, a full-bleed panel is

entirely appropriate. This panel would go right off the printed page in comic form, as opposed to being constricted inside a box.

Use several thumbnails if necessary to get the look of the page working. They should only take a minute or two at most, and are minutes well spent.

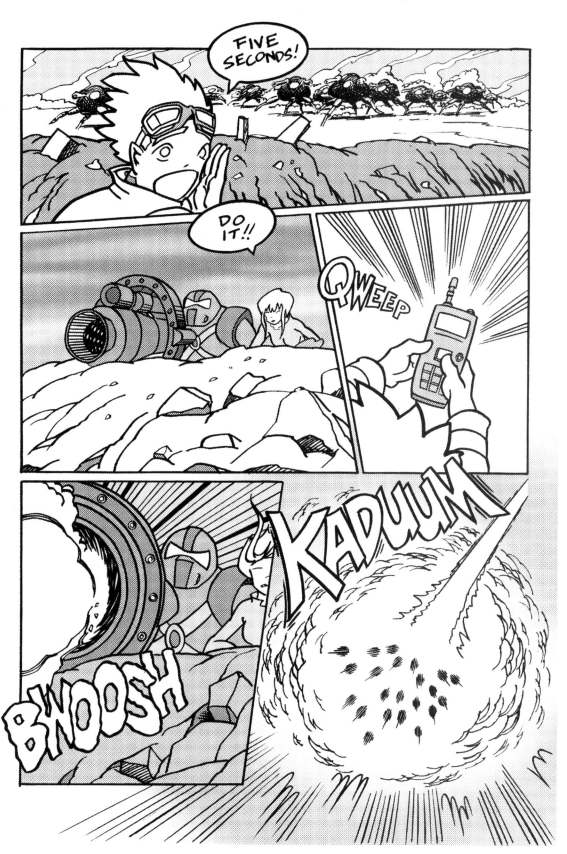

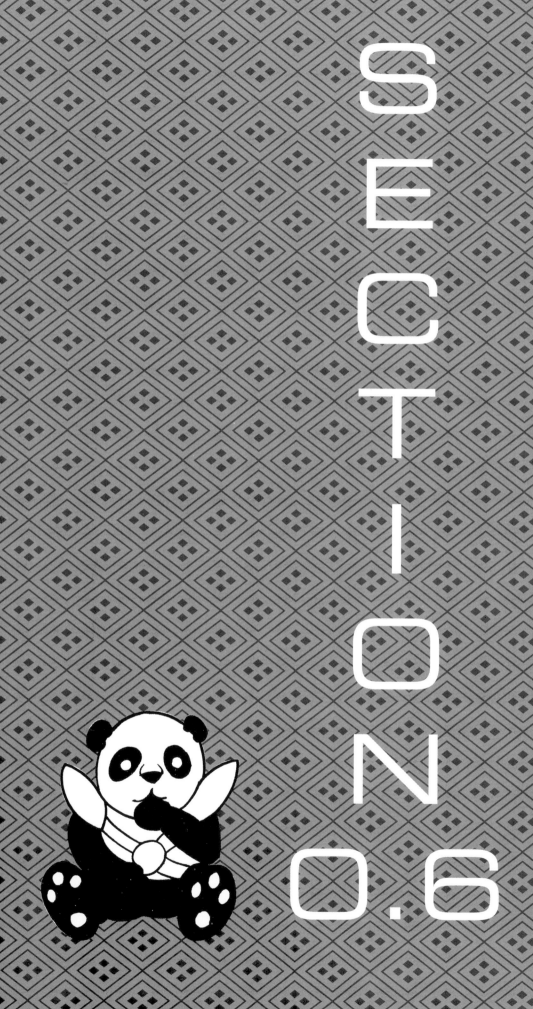

SECTION 0.6

Personality crisis

Often, page after page of Manga has almost nothing but characters on it.

Characters present a different kind of problem for the Manga creator. This isn't simply a question of learning the rules; our own understanding of people, or for that matter animals, behavior, reactions and motivations, have to be introduced.

Character creation usually begins with the idea of an archetype. This is a particular type of character with one powerful and clearly defined characteristic. Here are some examples: the coward, the miser, the wise man, the temptress, the trickster, the misery, the clown, the idiot, the genius. Try coming up with a few of your own, then doodle character sketches which capture these archetypes.

Needless to say, these archetypes are just a starting point. If the characters are naked expressions of these types, they will come across as blunt and unengaging.

This chapter takes several very different characters, and using both images and words, rounds them out to create fully-formed, ready-for-action personalities.

We'll see all of these characters in full character rotation, model sheets and preliminary drawings, showing us the stages they went through.

But first let's get to grips with the essence of what makes a well-formed character.

Sharper focus

What separates a good character from a great one? The following are several factors which can have a big impact on a character's success:

- originality
- visual appeal
- believability
- context

ORIGINALITY: a character which is little more than an agglomeration of clichés is hardly likely to set the world on fire. One of the notable aspects of Manga is that almost anything is acceptable as a character. If you want to have a bionic pumpkin, then go for it. A three hundred year old woman whose body sprouts killer eels? Why not? As long as you can work it into a plot and make it entertaining, you can do what you like.

VISUAL APPEAL: as well as being well-designed, a character should ideally have defining visual characteristics. These act almost as symbols which immediately identify the character to the reader. They don't have to be pretty or slick, they can be downright ugly or just plain bizarre. A good example of this is when we create a team. A team has to look simultaneously similar and different. At right is the team of "Blackberry Stranger" to explain:

BELIEVABILITY: contrary to what you might at first think, this doesn't mean "could this character really exist?". What it means is "does this character have enough characteristics from the real world for us to be able to relate to him/her/it?" Dialogue and physical make-up are key points here.

CONTEXT: this means the right character for the right situation, or the right company. It also refers to the chemistry that exists as they bring each other's characters into sharper focus.

Not all errors of context are as obvious as the picture above. Every context or scenario has its own parameters and possibilities. Move much outside these and the mood and context become undermined.

Dialogue

It's instructive to visit your local mall, café or sports game and actually listen to the way people discuss things. It's very rare that people speak to each other directly, answer each other's questions without deviation, or even by asking another question. This is because what is taking place is a spontaneous, unpredictable exchange.

Often the first and most important mistake made when writing dialogue for characters is the failure to use language to bring out character traits.

Manga tends to be less dialogue-heavy than Western comic art, but just a small amount of poor dialogue can ruin the flow of an otherwise enjoyable story.

There are two extremes which should also be avoided. At one extreme is the cliché; tired words that add nothing and detract considerably by displaying a lack of imagination. It is possible to use cliché deliberately, for instance, to demonstrate the unoriginality of a character's thought patterns, but even this has to be done creatively to succeed. At the other end there is pretentiousness, or a deliberate and obvious attempt to appear smarter than we are.

The creator should always remain invisible. The writer's sudden or obvious presence is jarring and an obstruction to the smooth flow of a story. If it is well told at the right pace, the reader will forget that they are reading the product of another's mind.

The fact that the vast majority of manga we read has been translated from Japanese should not go unmentioned. Translation is a real skill and unless we speak the original language it's almost impossible to tell how well the job's been done by the translator. Occasionally, the dialogue has been translated straight from the Japanese, with no allowances for Western modes of dialogue. The results of this are often plain bizarre or even hilarious, the anime show *Galaxy Angel* being a prime example. All of this has fed in to the lexicon of Western manga, giving it a feel and vocabulary distinct from other comics.

150

Character development

The following pages all follow the same formula, putting a character through their paces.

CHARACTER PAGE

This is where we discover the basic facts of the character. Making a page similar to this is a good way of reminding ourselves of the traits, motivations and circumstances of the person depicted.

PRELIMINARY DRAWINGS

The drawings on these pages show the character in development, from the basic first idea through to the final character. The differences between the drawing vary from character to character, depending on how quickly the characterization was realized. The "Pandam" character (featured on page 164) probably went through the most changes, starting life a little too much like a regular thick-set guy with a panda's head. What was needed was a bulkier, more lumbering appearance.

MODEL SHEETS

These are where the rules for the character are set in stone and are essential in anime, where the same character may be drawn by a number of different people. By using model sheets, we guarantee consistency. As we create page after page of Manga, we can, usually quite unconsciously, slip out of gear with our character without even realizing it. This often means a head drawn slightly too large or the nose too high. It's at times like

these that model sheets become indispensible tools.

CHARACTER ROTATIONS

Often called "turnarounds," these series of drawings give us the information we need to draw our character from any angle we need. Usually drawn at eye level with little or no perspective they take the guesswork out of a potentially awkward angle, thus saving us a lot of time and frustration.

The turnarounds are presented both as pencil construction drawings and as finished line art. There are six drawings and not the eight that you may expect. This is because the final two are basically mirror images of rotations two and three.

Take one of your own characters and put it through this rotation series.

I've included characters large and small as well as both male and female. But it would take a whole book to cover anywhere near the possible range of shapes and sizes of possible characters. If you're stuck for ideas to try your own turnarounds out with, why not try it with one of the many other characters, vehicles etc in this book. Better still, take a character from your favorite manga title. Rather than simply copying the character, create a turnaround from the information you find on the pages. When you're happy with the result, make a few modifications of your own. Then a few more. In this way you will learn a huge amount about character construction and development.

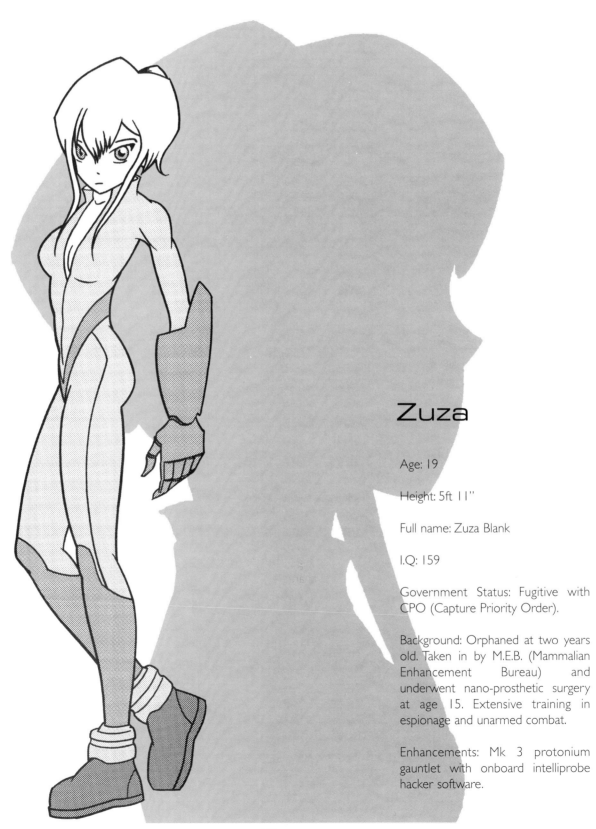

Zuza

Age: 19

Height: 5ft 11"

Full name: Zuza Blank

I.Q: 159

Government Status: Fugitive with CPO (Capture Priority Order).

Background: Orphaned at two years old. Taken in by M.E.B. (Mammalian Enhancement Bureau) and underwent nano-prosthetic surgery at age 15. Extensive training in espionage and unarmed combat.

Enhancements: Mk 3 protonium gauntlet with onboard intelliprobe hacker software.

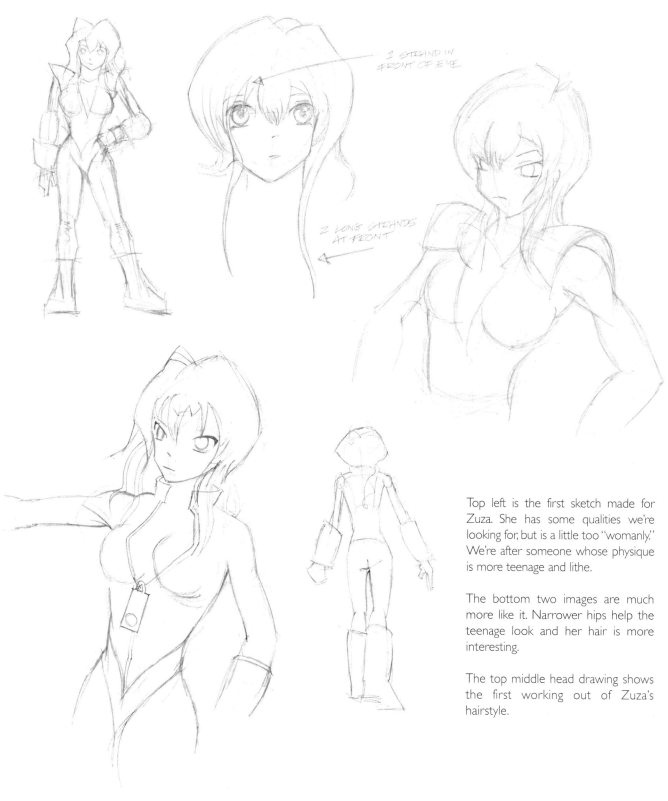

1 STRAND IN FRONT OF EYE

2 LONG STRANDS AT FRONT

Top left is the first sketch made for Zuza. She has some qualities we're looking for, but is a little too "womanly." We're after someone whose physique is more teenage and lithe.

The bottom two images are much more like it. Narrower hips help the teenage look and her hair is more interesting.

The top middle head drawing shows the first working out of Zuza's hairstyle.

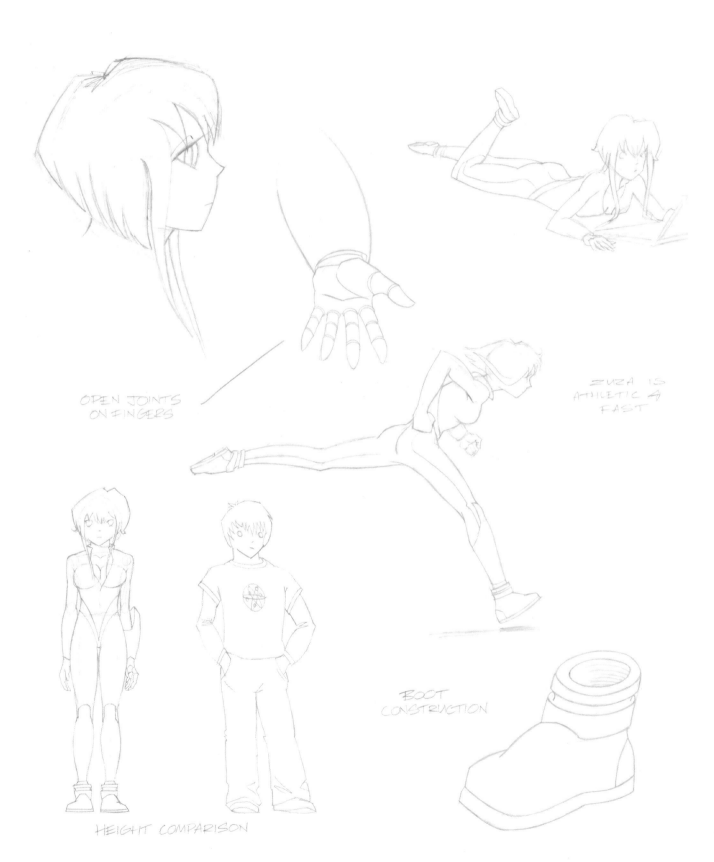

6

OPEN JOINTS
ON FINGERS

ZUZA IS
ATHLETIC &
FAST

HEIGHT COMPARISON

BOOT
CONSTRUCTION

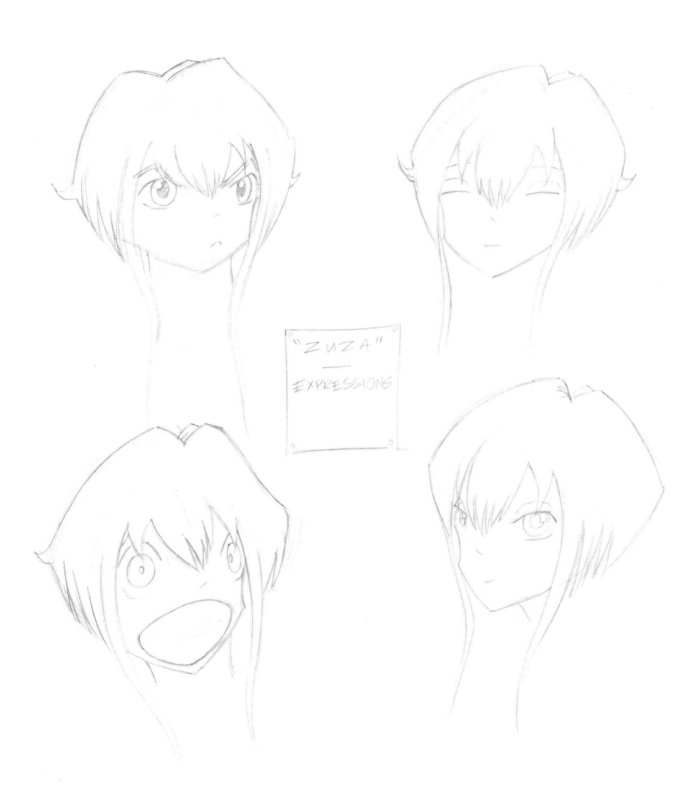

"ZUZA"
—
EXPRESSIONS

155

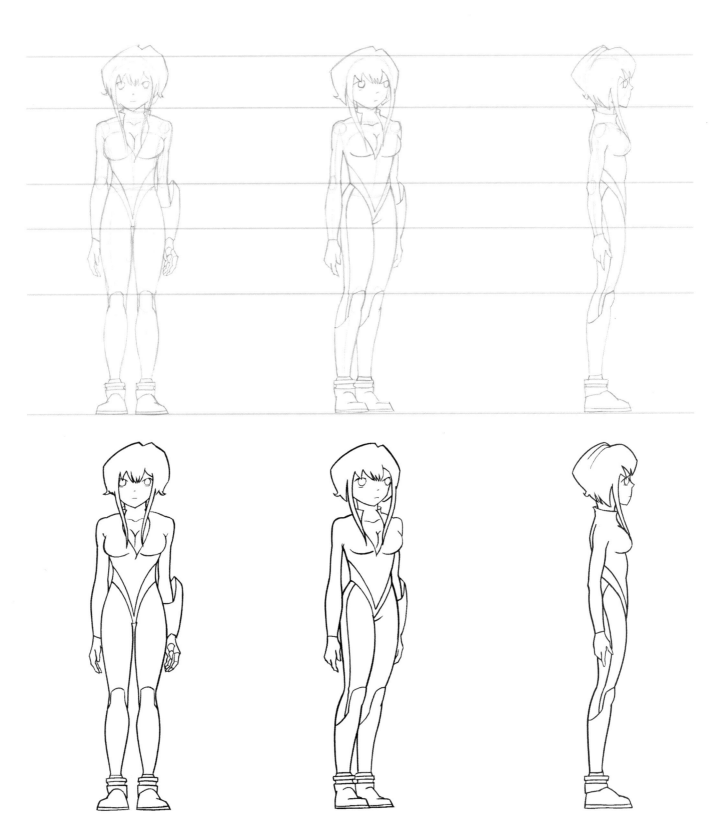

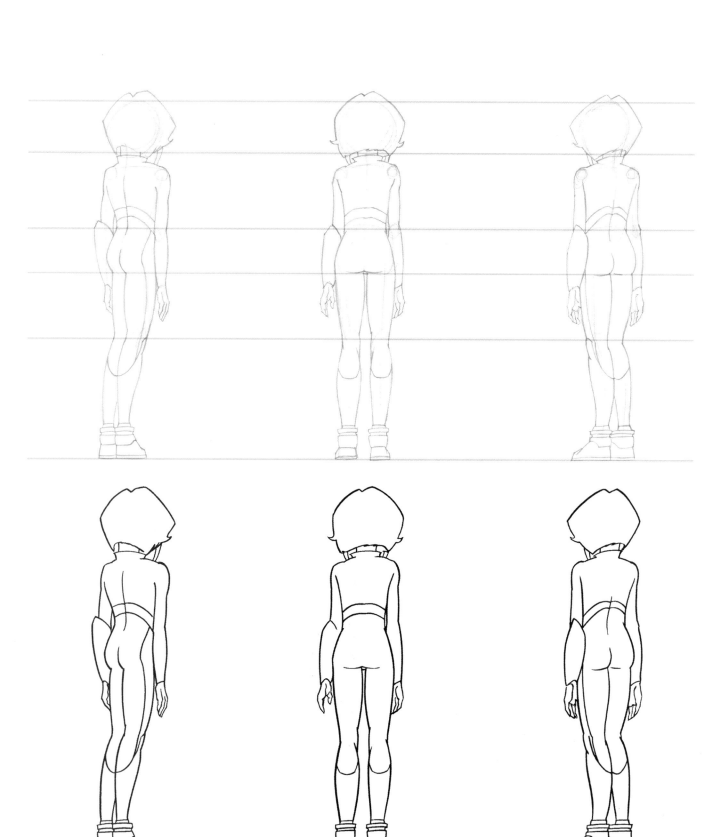

157

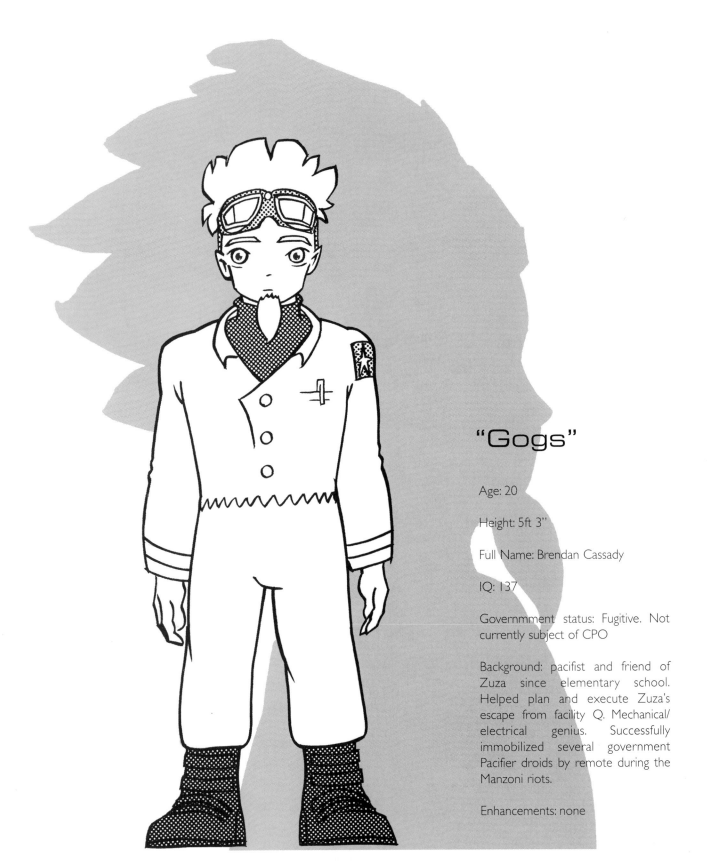

"Gogs"

Age: 20

Height: 5ft 3"

Full Name: Brendan Cassady

IQ: 137

Governmment status: Fugitive. Not currently subject of CPO

Background: pacifist and friend of Zuza since elementary school. Helped plan and execute Zuza's escape from facility Q. Mechanical/ electrical genius. Successfully immobilized several government Pacifier droids by remote during the Manzoni riots.

Enhancements: none

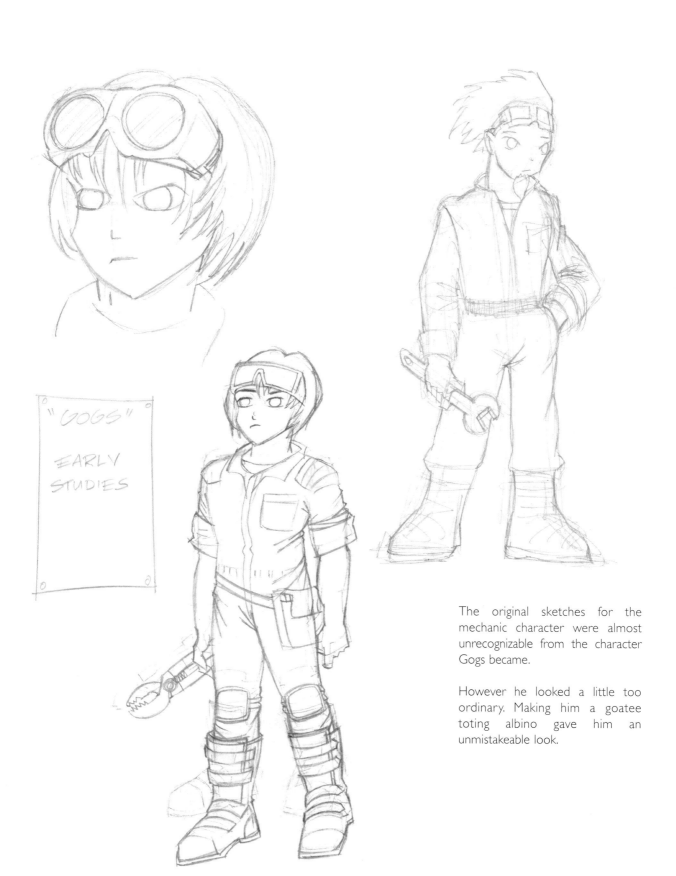

"GOGS"

EARLY STUDIES

The original sketches for the mechanic character were almost unrecognizable from the character Gogs became.

However he looked a little too ordinary. Making him a goatee toting albino gave him an unmistakeable look.

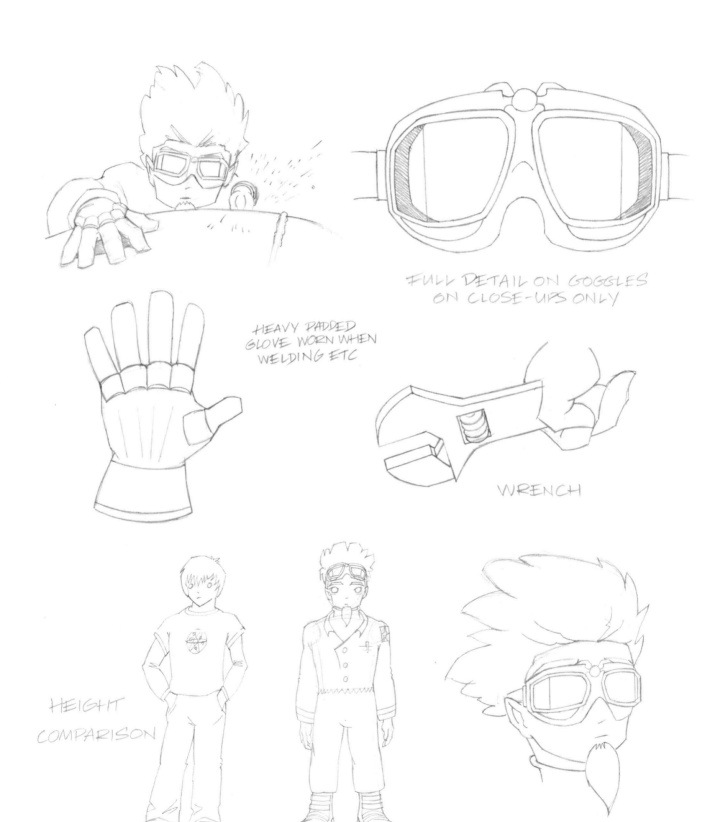

FULL DETAIL ON GOGGLES
ON CLOSE-UPS ONLY

HEAVY PADDED
GLOVE WORN WHEN
WELDING ETC

WRENCH

HEIGHT
COMPARISON

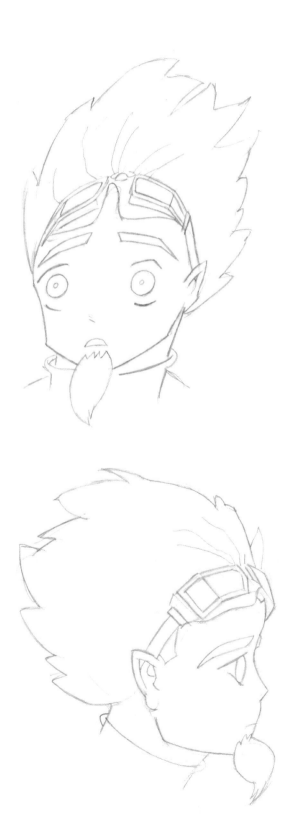

"GOGS"

EXPRESSIONS

161

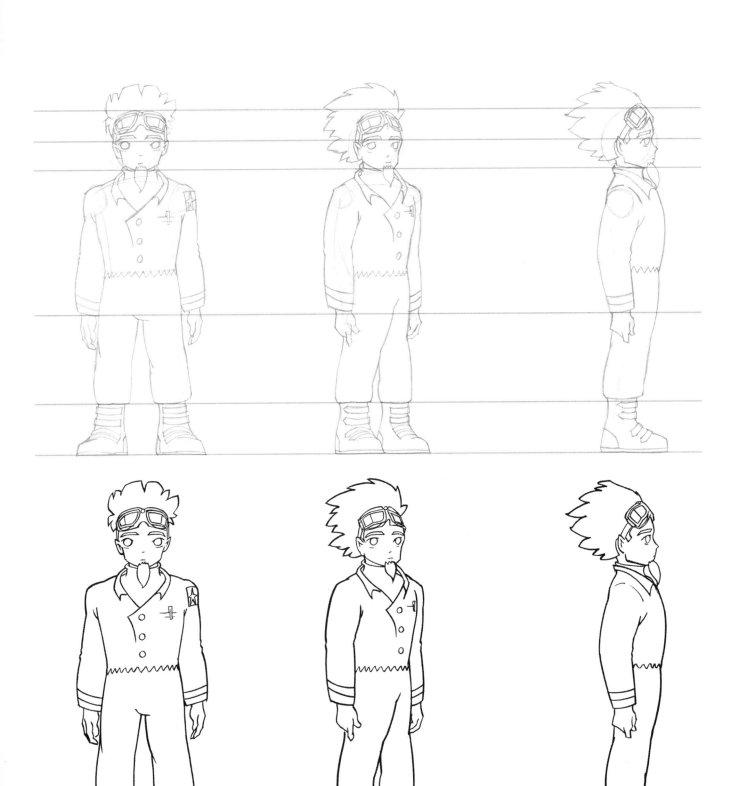

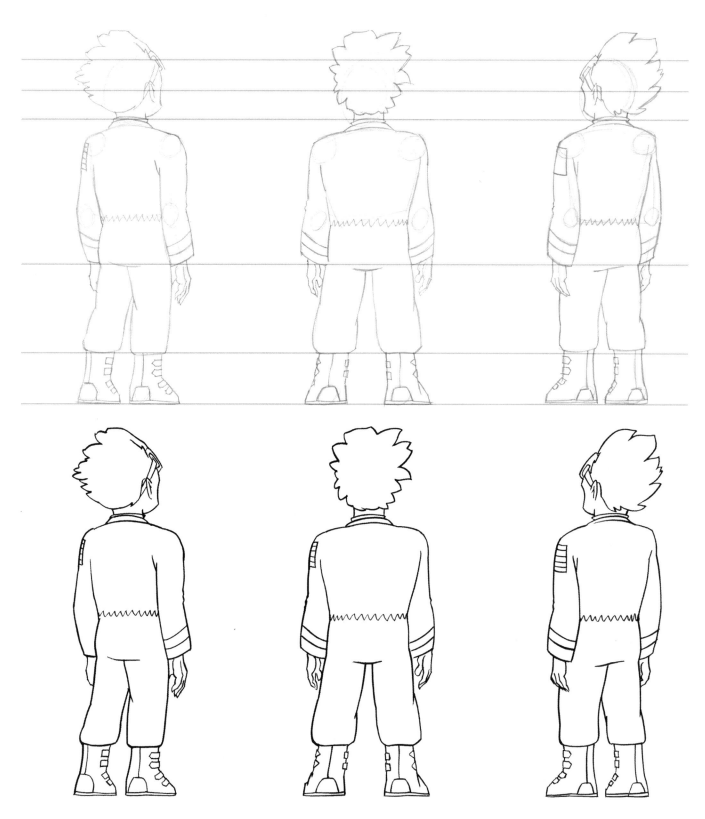

163

Pandam-3J

Age: 11/28

Height: 6ft 1''

Full name: Pandam-3J

IQ: 132

Government status: Missing, declared destroyed.

Background: Pandam-3J is the result of MEB's ground-breaking work in cross-species enhancement. After a string of costly and largely fatal experiments, the first successful mind-transplant was performed between a human and a panda.

Enhancements: Almost every aspect of Pandam-3J, save the head, has received enhancement.

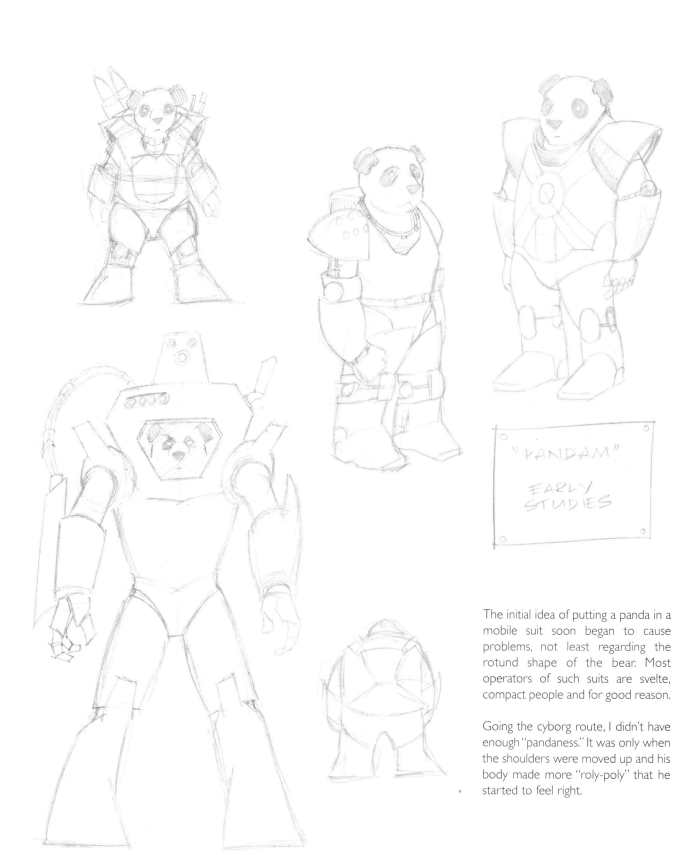

"PANDAM"

EARLY STUDIES

The initial idea of putting a panda in a mobile suit soon began to cause problems, not least regarding the rotund shape of the bear. Most operators of such suits are svelte, compact people and for good reason.

Going the cyborg route, I didn't have enough "pandaness." It was only when the shoulders were moved up and his body made more "roly-poly" that he started to feel right.

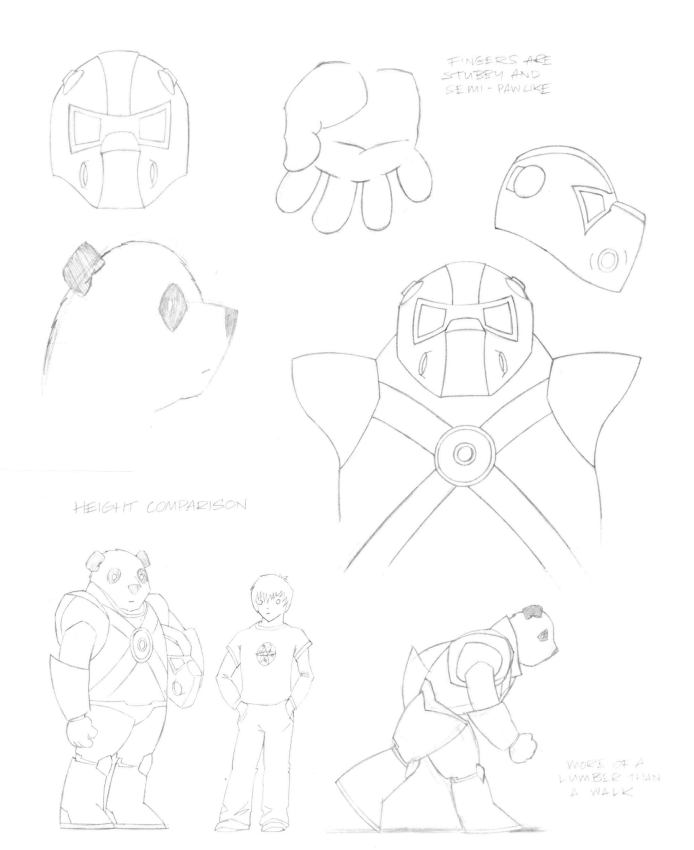

FINGERS ARE
STUBBY AND
SEMI-PAWLIKE

HEIGHT COMPARISON

MORE OF A
LUMBER THAN
A WALK

"PANDAM"

EXPRESSIONS

PANDAM IS SURPRISINGLY
EXPRESSIVE FOR A PANDA.
HIS HUMAN BRAIN DEMANDS
IT, THOUGH IT OFTEN HURTS.

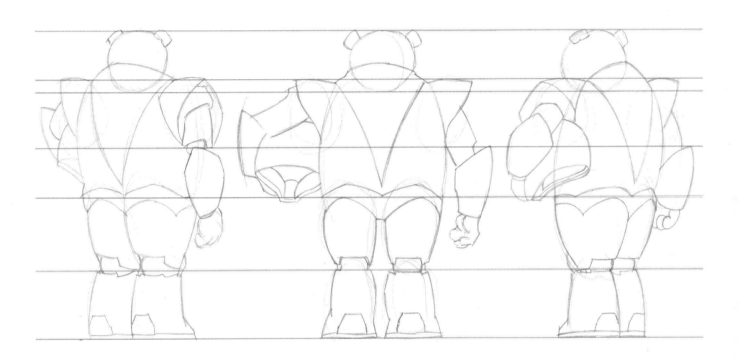

Tomoko

Age: Unknown

Height: 3ft 2"

Full Name: Tomoko Takahashi

IQ: 168

Government Status: Unknown

Background: Any attempts to lure information out of this tiny, super-smart girl/lady have been in vain. Refuses to discuss any aspect of the past, even what happened yesterday. Mans the controls at Monkeypop Terminal with unerring authority.

Enhancements: unknown

"TOMOKO"

EARLY STUDIES

More than any of the other characters, Tomoko arrived on the paper almost fully formed. She needed a traditional but timeless feel, as well as an aura of playful mystery.

Billie Holiday came to mind when the single lotus in the hair was added. Sometimes if something works, why question it?

171

LOTUS
CONSTRUCTION

HEIGHT COMPARISON

"TOMOKO"

EXPRESSIONS

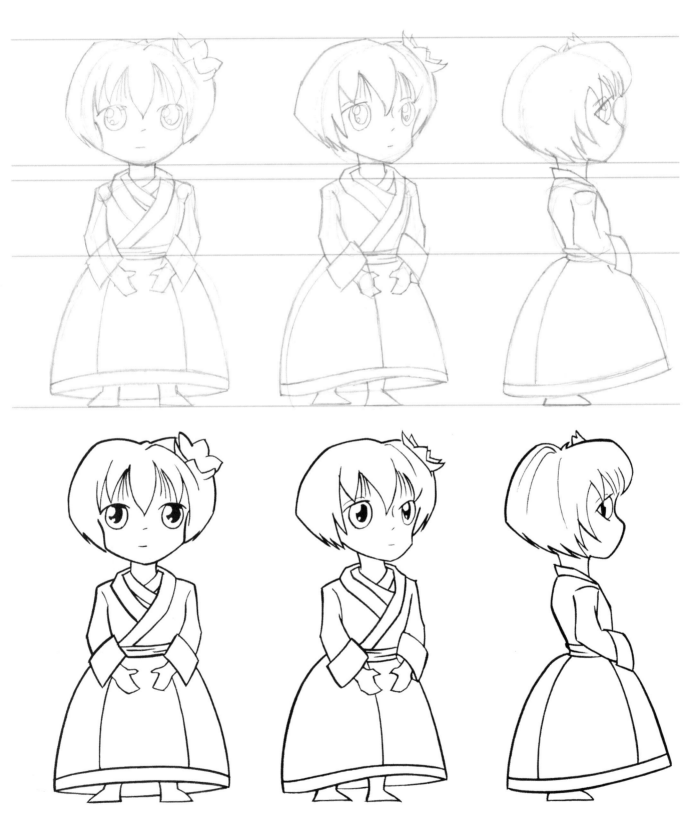

174

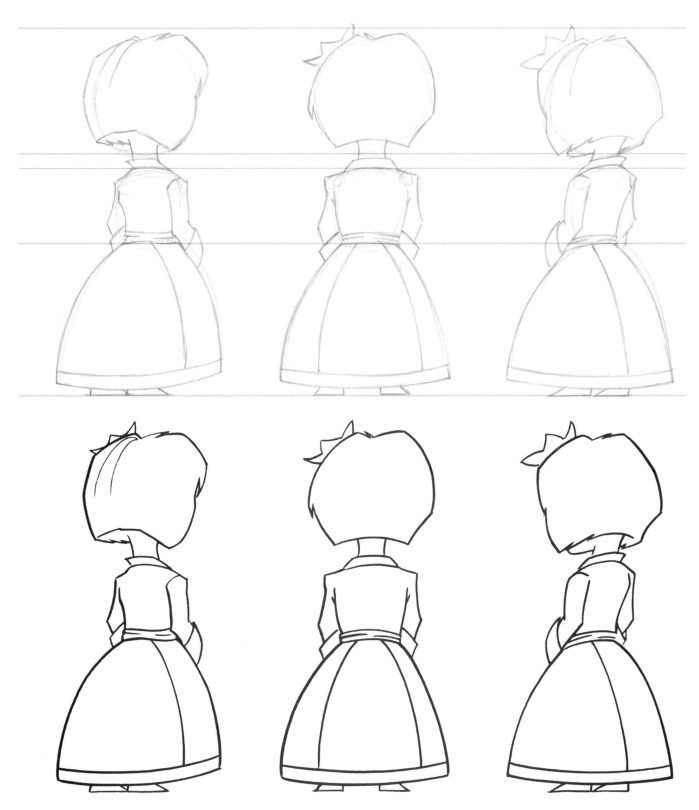

Zarkoz

Age: 32

Height: 7ft 3''

Full name: Geoff Mussorsky

IQ: 118

Government status: Fugitive with a CPO out

Background: the horned thing that was once Geoff Mussorsky is the result of illegal abuse of equipment and facilities inside MEB by an over-ambitious bioneer. Although terryfing, his look is acheived purely through bio-tech. Mussorsky has lost his mind and is convinced he is Zarkoz, Lord of the Damned.

Enhancements: numerous

176

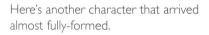

"ZARKOZ"
EARLY
STUDIES

Here's another character that arrived almost fully-formed.

When you need a real powerful basket-case type, there's nothing quite like a pair of big, fat horns to say "evil."

The first draft at top left didn't quite have that hugeness so the shoulders were widened and he was generally bulked out.

The cloven tootsies were just too good to resist.

HEIGHT COMPARISON

"ZARKOZ"

EXPRESSIONS

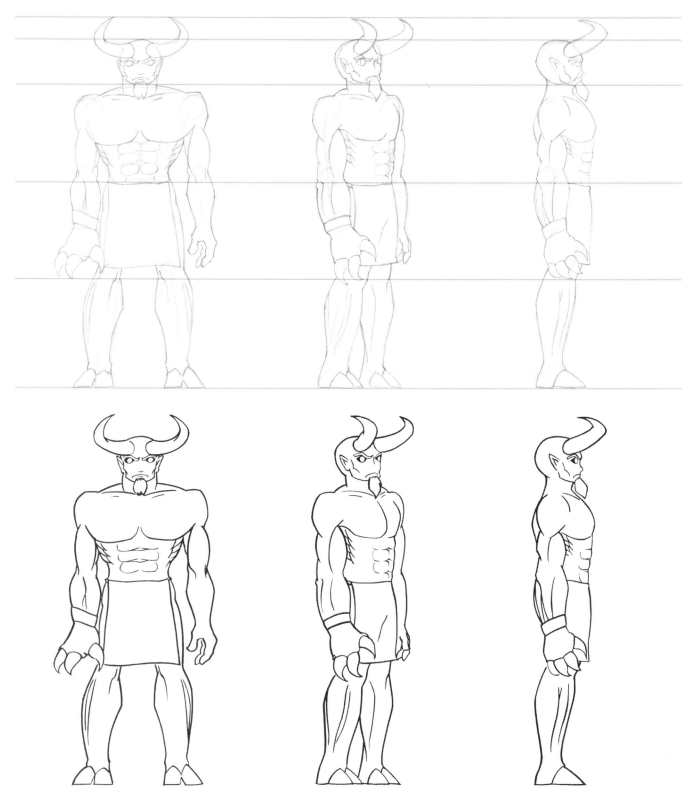

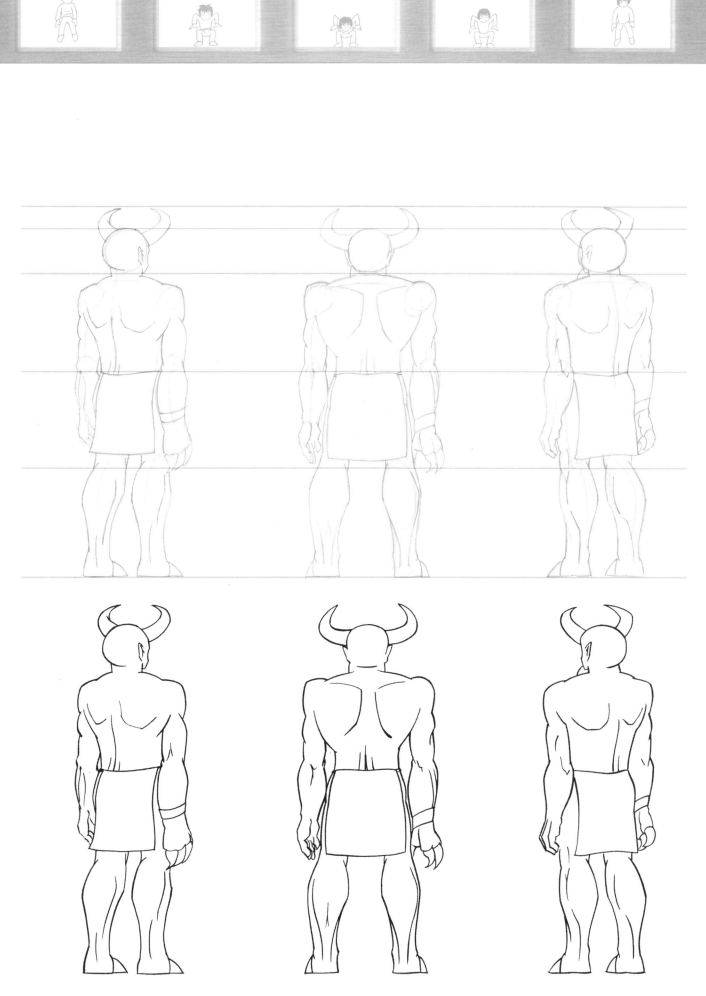

Size comparisons

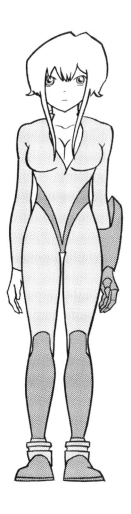

The previous pages should have given an idea of the height and size of each character compared with Joe Average. But there's nothing better than seeing the family of characters all together for the first time. Tomoko is lucky if she's one-quarter of the size of Zarkoz.

By following all of the guidelines in this chapter, we'll find that having put our characters through all of these various development methods, they'll have a life of their own. Fresh ideas about who they really are will occur almost without thinking. One idea tends to suggest another, starting an almost endless flow of possibilities.

The more work we do on a character, the more we get to know them. Their personalities are expressed through their appearance. We begin to instinctively know what they would do, how they would react given any situation. Once we arrive at this point, a story involving these characters will almost write itself.

We hope this chapter and indeed this book has given you some new ideas and approaches to lifting your Manga to the next level.

I know we're in serious jeopardy of repeating ourselves here, but really, you won't get much practical use out of this book without the one thing essential to your own progress: practice!

If you're really serious about Manga, you should aim to get yourself some professional work as soon as you think you might be ready for it. This is not to encourage people to rush into full-time drawing before they are ready for it. It's just that there is absolutely no substitute for the real business of having to deliver work on a very real, and often tight, schedule. If you can deal with the pressure this often entails, you will find that this is the very best and ultimately only way to get the most out of your abilities. Very few of us can push ourselves the way a real deadline can. Until we do this, we never really find out what we are made of.

May your creative visions be made real, and may your pencil line flow with the confidence of the greatest Manga-kas!

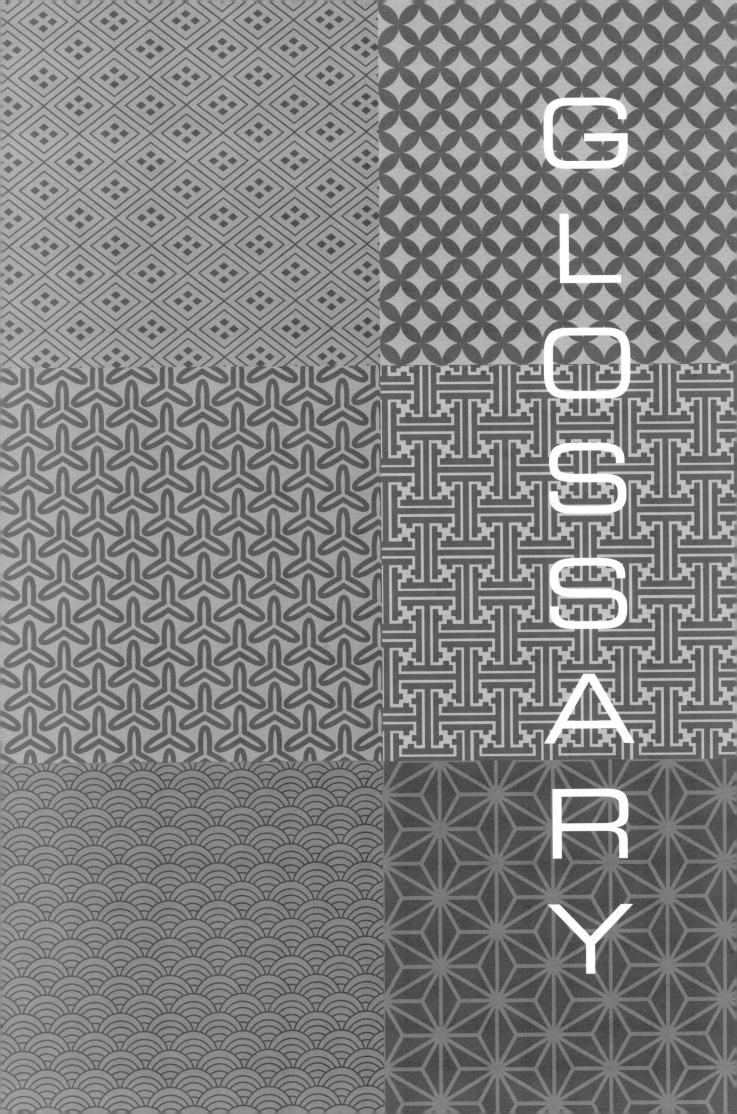

GLOSSARY

Terms worth knowing

ANIME – the animated form of Manga, sometimes referred to as "Japanimation." The mechanical needs and restrictions of animators and colorists mean anime is often less visually extreme than pure Manga. That said, anime is often the product of the adaptation of existing Manga, *Akira* and *Ghost in the Shell* being obvious examples. Whether a full-length feature or a ten-minute tv show, the name is applicable to either.

BITMAP – a color mode which represents images as a collection of small black dots. In bitmap mode, only black or white can be represented. See pages 95-97 for more details.

BRISTOL BOARD – also called Bristol Paper, depending on the guage. The preferred paper type for serious illustrators and Manga-kas. It has a super-smooth drawing surface and is relatively bleedproof provided the surface hasn't had an eraser applied.

DOUJINSHI – roughly the equivalent of fanzines in the West, this type of Manga is produced by amateurs and has provided a way for many Manga artists to get their first exposure. The literal meaning of this term is roughly "same material, different people."

DPI – dots per inch. The amount of dots or pixels used for every inch of an image is what determines the resolution or quality of the final image.

FULL BLEED – the bleed of any image refers to the area outside that which is intended to be printed.

When an image is said to be *full bleed*, the image to be printed extends beyond the edge of the printed paper, i.e. the finished, printed image has no border. This book's cover is an example of full bleed.

HENSHIN – the transformation of a character into his or her alter ego

HENTAI – an "adults only" form of anime, usually depicting scenes of sexual indecency.

KAWAI – a commonly used Manga term meaning *"cute."*

MANGA – first coined by celebrated artist Hokusai in the 19th century, the term nowadays refers to any printed visual storytelling, gags and so on, which have their origin in Japan. A Manga artist is called a *manga-ka*.

MECHA – a shortened version of the word mechanical or mechanoid. This can refer to characters humanoid or otherwise, or highly mechanized vehicles etc.

OTAKU – though literally meaning *maniac*, in Manga and anime circles this refers to a person with a serious obsession with the form.

RENSAI – a serialized story. Like Western comics, these can either be limited to several issues or can run for many years.

SEINEN MANGA – when boys outgrow shounen Manga (see below) this is the type of Manga they would gravitate towards as an alternative. This type features more mature themes and is aimed at male audiences of 18 and over.

SHOUJO MANGA – this type of Manga is created for a target audience of young girls, *Sailor Moon* being a typical example.

SHOUNEN MANGA – like the above, but created for boys. *Dragonball Z* is a prime example of this type.

SUPER DEFORMED – this style of drawing is commonplace in Manga and is usually used to denote extreme reactions of characters. Normally tiny mouths can expand to the size of basketballs, given the right situation.

TANBI KEI or YAOI – although this branch of Manga features young, gay men, much of the audience for this *boy's love* type is young women.

TANKOUBON – this book format Manga is usually used to compile collections of several issues of Manga. Masamune Shirow's *Appleseed* was a rare exception, as it was published first in Tankoubon without appearing first as a serialized Manga. The Western equivalent would be the graphic novel collection.

TONE SHEET – an adhesive backed transparent sheet used for adding patterns or shades of grey to Manga. Like a *bitmap* image, these patterns or tones are composed of black dots, lines etc, and help add texture and depth to Manga images.

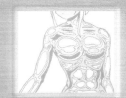

Anime worth viewing

The following list is a small sampling of what we consider to be essential anime:

AKIRA – a groundbreaking film which established feature length anime on the world stage. New heights of visual sophistication were reached in this 1986 release.

BLOOD THE LAST VAMPIRE – among the best examples of gothic horror, with great looking lighting and color design.

BUBBLEGUM CRISIS – a good example of common Manga themes, especially body suits and action a plenty.

COWBOY BEBOP – smart tales of bounty hunting both terrestrial and spacebound. Great soundtrack and a dirty, gritty urban environment.

GALAXY ANGEL – translated straight from the Japanese, this series has to be the most surreal out there. Flying meat buns and spaceships masquerading as giant diet machines à la *Solaris* are among the more ordinary elements of this wigged out kids show.

GRAVE OF THE FIREFLIES – a Studio Ghibli production, this has to rank as one of the most traumatic and heartbreaking animes ever. The opening gambit of this anime is the grim, desolate death of the lead character – and that's just for openers.

GHOST IN THE SHELL – the new benchmark in anime when it was released in the mid-nineties. Amazing cybernetics and stunning backgrounds combine with a thought-provoking plot to make one of the best anime features ever.

KITE – this dark story is not for children. However, it is a beautifully told tale with anything but a Hollywood ending.

MACROSS – a visual feast, this series deals with themes of war, but in a gentle and intelligent way. Great flying transforming vehicles and Macross' use of magic is among the best in the field.

NEON GENESIS EVANGELION – more than just a showcase for collosal mecha, this show is brimming with original ideas and characters. Not least of which are an intelligent penguin who lives in a fridge.

NINJA SCROLL – set in feudal Japan and astonishing in its brutality, this series takes the prize for the biggest, nastiest villains in the history of anime. If you're upset by having characters built up in your affections, only to see them torn asunder in the most violent way imaginable, this series is definitely not for you.

NOIR – with *James Bond* style graphics at the opening credits and a Paris setting, this series follows the activities of an elite group of asassins. But killing isn't easy or remotely fun, as this intellectually rewarding show aims to demonstrate.

PATLABOR – notable primarily for its inventiveness in mobile suit creation.

The Patlabors are huge, human piloted police enforcement mechas.

PERFECT BLUE – dark and sublime, this realistic anime is hard to describe without giving too much away. Disturbing. Highly recommended.

PRINCESS MONONOKE – directed by Haiyo Miyazaki at the height of his powers. A very singular way of looking at the impact of man's progress on nature. Great animal studies and a profoundly spiritual story.

SPIRITED AWAY – again, Miyazaki at his best. This surreal tale concerns the rites of passage of a miserable, self-absorbed girl as she is forced into hard labor in the most bizarre washhouse ever. Radish spirits, dragons and animated coal-dust creatures abound in this storytelling tour-de-force.

Studio Ghibli have produced many of the highest quality animes out there. All of them are worth seeing, but as well as the above, check out *Kiki's Delivery Service*, *Porco Rosso*, *Nausicaa*, *Laputa* and *My Neighbor Totoro*.

All the above should be readily available with English language tracks. That said, the dubbed English can be less than faithful to the original. Sometimes it's preferable to have the original Japanese language track and use the English subtitles.

Manga worth reading

The following is a short list of Manga creators worthy of note. Their particular strengths are listed in order to help the reader get inspiration when tackling specific techniques and forms.

KIA ASAMIYA

Best known for *Silent Mobius*, a storyline featuring a demon-hunting special police group, Asamiya's work is particularly worth checking out for explosive energy fields, powerfully drawn demons and nocturnal urban landscapes.

HAIYO MIYAZAKI

Probably the greatest living anime director, Miyazaki has produced plenty of Manga too. His densely drawn *Nausicaa of the Valley of the Wind* started life as a Manga before its anime production in 1984 and is his major Manga work. Much of Miyazaki's other Manga is rendered in pure watercolor.

TSUTOMU NIHEI

The creator of *Blame*, this Manga-ka started out as a trainee architect. Not surprisingly, the buildings in *Blame* are among the best examples found in Manga. As all the action is set in a post apocalyptic subterranea, the atmospheres created are dark, future gothic and sumptuous.

TAKESHI OBATA

Amongst the most technically brilliant of Manga artists, Obata's Manga *Hikaru No Go* started a massive craze for the game "Go" among elementary schoolkids.

KATSUHIRO OTOMO

The creator of the legendary *Akira*, Otomo has an impressive arsenal of techniques. His vehicles, both invented and real are always beautifully rendered. If you ever need to see how billowing clouds of smoke should be drawn, look no further than Otomo.

MASAMUNE SHIROW

One of the giants of modern Manga, Shiro is the creator of *Appleseed*, *Ghost in the shell* and *Dominion*, among others. His stories tend to revolve around the relationships between society, technology and government. Look at his work when you need to see how motor vehicles, collapsed bulidings and interiors should be done.

OSAMA TEZUKA

Universally acclaimed as the "God of Manga," Tezuka did more than anyone to establish and develop the modern Manga form. His work first came to the attention of the West in the 1960s when his *Astro Boy* anime began its screening on American TV. Among his best known works is *Black Jack* which concerns the cases of a brilliant but maverick surgeon. His first work, *Diary of Ma-chan* was published in 1946.

RUMIKO TAKAHASHI

The creator of the much-loved and long-running Manga series *Ranma 1/2*, Takahashi is probably the best known female Manga-ka. Her stories are playful, magical and bizarre, often featuring strange human-to-animal transformations. Although these defy all logic, her skill as a storyteller transcends such concerns, as the reader is taken on a journey of pure fun.

HONORABLE MENTIONS:

MAKI KUSUMOTO – *Kiss xxx*. High design and heavy use of intense light.

JUNJI ITO – dreamlike and sinister, some of the strangest Manga you will see.

RYOICHI IKEGAMI – *Crying Freeman*. Ikegami has worked in a wide variety of styles, all beautifully drawn.

KOGE DONBO – if you want to make a study of Manga eyes, Donbo is as good a place to start as any.

AKIRA TORIYAMA – not just *Dragonball*, Toriyama produces great cartoon style manga such as *Sandland* and *Dr Slump*.

TSUKASA HOJO – *City Hunter*, *Cat's Eye*. If you like your Manga in a realistic style Hojo is one of the best.

TAIYO MATSUMOTO – *Ping-Pong*. The page layouts in Matsumoto's table-tennis Manga are among the most radical around.

JUNKO MIZUNO – *Pure Trance*. Cute characters doing things they really shouldn't. Strangely 1960s looking.

MASAMI YUUKI – *Patlabor*. Some of the best dynamic figure drawing you will see.

Drawing exercises

We began this book with an artistic warm-up, drawing circles and figures of eight. We'll end with a summary of useful exercises. Little and often is our motto. Spend between 30 minutes to an hour every day working through the basics. If you need encouragement keep the first page you ever do and at the end of one month compare it with the newest.

Firstly, let's look at linework. Loosen up with circles and figures of eight. When you feel bored, finish with some single line drawings. See how close you can get to perfection.

Here's another seemingly unexciting but really beneficial exercise. Take a large sheet of paper and draw long, straight lines across it. Keep them as parallel as possible. This will help you gain confidence in your line and train your hand/eye coordination.

Vary the medium every day. Start with your familiar pencil or ballpoint. Then branch out to a variety of different types to get a feel for these as well. When you become more confident you can move to dip pen or brush.

Like limbering up for some strenuous physical activity you are now comfortable and ready for action. From here you can go in many directions, but quick drawings will be better than protracted studies.

It's important to strike a balance between observational drawing and that which is created from our imagination.

Draw a couple of pages of very quick figure sketches straight from your head. Now do the same thing but working from the television. Don't let concious thought get in the way. Let the information flow from eye to hand. If you're worried about the result you're doing it wrong. Do this until it's mindless. What we are drawing, or how good it looks is not important; the process of doing it is.

Now you should be ready to begin. You can start with a still life or go out and observe people.

The chosen medium will to some extent dictate the approach.

If you are interested in improving your tonal work use charcoal and a putty rubber. Either cover the entire sheet in charcoal and remove the highlights with the rubber, or build up the shadows straight in charcoal. Alternatively you could work with black and white acrylic and a thick brush, or watercolor/ink washes. There are no rules, work out what you wish to achieve and think about the best approach.

If you need to concentrate on your linework try a variety of different pens, pencils etc, each will have a strength and weakness.

Experimentation will make your personal artistic journey that much more rewarding.

What and how you draw will also bring different results. Find what you are weakest at and target that. Just drawing the things you're already good at will keep you going round in circles.

Still life drawing, if approached correctly, need not be boring. It's entirely up to you whether it's dull or not. Arrange simple objects, light them in a challenging way, make some rough preliminary sketches, then make a final drawing. The primary consideration here is composition, how you arrange the images on the page. Why does one arrangement work but another seem uninteresting?

The method you use will dictate what you get from the drawing. Tonal value, line, perspective and mood are all examples of aspects worth exploring. But you should have a strong idea about what exactly your aims are.

If you are finding perspective difficult take a plumbline and a ruler, as described in chapter 2. Hold the ruler out in front of you along the edge of a line we can see such as the edge of a book case, and compare the plumbline angle with the ruler. Transfer the ruler's angle directly to the page. If you are sufficiently careful, you should be able to build up an accurate version of the scene before you. In this way, you can begin to get the fundamentals of perspective permanently lodged in your mind.

Work out what your needs are and then tailor the methods in this book to those needs. If you concentrate mercilessly on your weak spots and temporarily suspend your desire to produce fully finished Manga, you'll quickly have the power to draw anything you choose without fear or difficulty.

Suminagashi

Commonly known as *marbling* in the English speaking world. This is a technique that is used for creating backgrounds throughout a broad range of Manga.

You will need:
Aluminium sulphate (alum)
Carrageenan or methcel
A large shallow tray
Eye droppers
Acrylic paints or inks
A comb, tooth picks, etc.

First you need to prepare a working area, preferably near a sink. Spread newspaper over your work surface and place your shallow tray on this. Do the same with another surface for drying the finished work, excluding the tray.

Next prepare the water. Try your local tap water. If this fails to produce good results try bottled water. Distilled water is the safest as certain minerals in water can adversely effect the process.

You need to make what is known as "size." This is the thick water on which the colored inks will float. If possible you should make this several hours before you begin. Slowly add the carrageenan or methcel to warm water, about a handful per gallon. Mix this in the tray with water about two inches deep. Leave this to gain thickness, the longer the better.

While you're waiting for this you can prepare the paper. You need to treat the surface in order for the colors to adhere on contact. Take about an eighth of a cup of alum and dissolve

slowly in a litre of water. You'll find it easier to use warm water to do this and then allow it to cool to room temperature. Next, sponge it onto your paper, cover the surface thoroughly, and leave it to dry.

It is important not to get the paper too wet as it may warp when drying. Good quality paper is recommended, because this can help eliminate any deformation.

Now the fun can begin.

The paints or inks should be about the consistency of whole milk. Choose your favorite colors and put them in a collection of pots each with their own eye droppers by the tray.

You'll need to float the paint on the size. Take the dropper and very carefully lay the ink drops on the surface. If the size is thick enough then the ink should spead out in a small circle. Normally we do this with a variety of colors to produce multicolor swirls, but it will work just as well with black and white.

There are traditional colors and patterns that have been repeated over the centuries. If you want to find out more there are numerous books and websites detailing these. It is probably best to do some simple experiments first so you can get some feel for this craft before attempting anything too ambitious.

This is where the comb, tooth picks, etc, come into play. Choose your tool and gently swirl the inks. Keep playing until you get something that appeals.

Moving the image from the size to the paper can be tricky. Try to bend the paper so that the middle touches the surface first, then let the ends roll out so that it lies flat on the liquid. The biggest enemies at this point are air bubbles which can keep the ink from the paper. After a few seconds, take the two corners furthest from you and try to peel the paper off the water.

Hopefully you will now have created a beautiful image. Gently rinse it in cold water to remove any excess size. You can now leave it to dry.

Cleaning the size is simple. Lay some porous paper, an old newspaper for instance, on any remaining areas of ink and then lift it out of the tray.

Now you can begin again with the ink drops. As with every craft, the more you experiment and persevere the more your work will improve.

Fair warning: Doing your own Suminagashi can be just too fascinating. You may find yourself spending far more time on this art than you spend on your Manga.

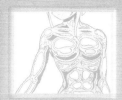

Appreciation

The following people made valuable contributions to the making of this book:

Mark Reynolds

Freelance illustrator and provider of the splendid images on pages 89, 91, 92 and 122.

Geoff Weeks

Professional modelmaker who kindly built the mecha seen on pages 114-116.

The following provided the soundtrack to the production of this book:

Kojima Mayumi, Elliott Smith, Cornelius, Mr Bungle, Miyazawa,

Robyn Hitchcock, Ed Harcourt, Thomas Dybdahl and Utah Phillips.

Thank you for keeping us almost sane.